WHEELS
and
DEALS

by Ian Thomas

in association with
Richard Frost

First published 2006 by

Pinegen Limited
95 Brighton Road, Surbiton Surrey KT6 5NF
Telephone: 020-8335 1100

© Pinegen Limited

ISBN 0-9552376-0-2

Origination by Pinegen Limited
Printed by Schmidt Grafisk Produktion in Denmark

Wheels and Deals

Foreword: by Barry Briggs, MBE

THOMMO was my dreaded promoter, business partner and mate around speedway for 20 plus years. I know that by agreeing to write this foreword for his book it is not going to be easy. It will be checked, rechecked and then he will want changes. Sorry Ian, this time I have the whip hand, no changes!

Thommo could have been an accountant. But to me he really is a frustrated would-be lawyer. He really loves the thought process and he would rather cross a minefield to win than take a safe helicopter ride. Nobody could write the speedway rulebook better than him.

When I rode for Hull I stayed overnight with Ian and Dorothy. I noticed on his bedside table the Speedway rulebook. I'm sure he brushed through it ever night. Sky television fans can see why, just watch a Belle Vue speedway match!

He cajoled (to deceive by flattery) me out of retirement. The decision wasn't too hard for me and Junie to decide, as I still loved racing.

Ian was 100 per cent right when he told me that you could not get a better speedway public to race in front of than the Hull people. But the track was a different story. Unfortunately I never did my homework on the Hull track properly before agreeing to sign.

It took two months of thrashing my head against a brick wall to realise that if you weren't leading after the first corner you were in trouble. I knew I was past my best, but for two months I diced with death for four laps each race trying to gain places. That was really the only minus of signing up with Thommo and Hull.

For the first time in my speedway life I was smart enough to build in a little comfort in my deal with Thommo for myself. Speedway is a tough life to have as a job, it is normally about the money in the bank. Once you deposit the money into your bank that is the end of the deal. But this time I took an object, something that I could feel and touch. I had a new Mercedes as a sign-on fee. It certainly helped after a frustrating night, or when you started to wonder why I was going through all the stress again. To just sit back into the luxury of Ian's generous gift made it bearable. But still after three years he was still calling it OUR car.

Hull was probably the most unusual season of my career. I was living in Germany and commuting to Hull for all of my meetings. The agreed deal to cover costs for air-fares to get me from Germany to England return proved impossible to meet. Thinking back I remember in the middle of our negotiations Ian's colleague left to check prices and deals with the local travel agent. I could never purchase any of these amazing deals – my mistake. Some small consolation was getting Ian (a night person) out of bed early to drive me to Manchester for my flight back to Germany.

Thommo was a silver-tongued devil and a couple of stories spring to mind and how he got me to do them still amazes me.

A cup meeting at Berwick that wasn't covered by our agreement was one. I didn't want to do it, but his pitch "I'll fly you up there and we will stay over-night at Lady so and so's Castle" was sinister enough to capture my imagination for another Thommo adventure. I rode badly, but my team-mates were fabulous that night. There was a Castle and a Lady but I think I could have done without the experience.

A Workington reunion was another case. This was Thommo at his very best. Bear in mind that Workington Speedway had been closed for 25 years. Thommo must have had a slack week and was in a creative mood. "Let's have a Workington reunion" he suggested and unbelievably a good crowd gathered.

Ian, the master showman, had the local television there. "Briggo do a bit for the TV will you, here put this jacket on," he said. Grumbling I retorted: "Ian this is a new jacket I'm wearing and I don't really want to wear that 'sign post' jacket.

Of course Ian had a deal with Wulfsport. All things are not bad, and the introduction to Bill Brown, Wulfsport's owner was a big bonus for me. Bill, his family and mine have been close friends ever since. Ian paid me for this two day Workington extravaganza, but with what? A free Wulfsport jacket of course!

The luxury Workington hotel was another story. "Briggo you might not realise this, but this Hotel is the Las Vegas of Cumbria," he told me. With great drama he threw back the threadbare curtains to prove this bold statement. Through the fog and gloom Workington Railway station was barely visible, as three of the five light bulbs had blown. Las Vegas? Yeah, we laughed and laughed.

Writing this foreword is my big and probably only chance to have a dig at our Thommo. So I can't possibly let the Hull pits saga pass without comment. When I rode for Hull, I was allotted my pit position. It was right next to the toilet and even today I don't think my toolbox looked like a toilet. But certainly the day after it smelled like one. At the time this didn't really bother me.

Three years later Ian signed Ivan Mauger to ride for Hull. Was Ivan allotted the same pits spot as Briggo? You must be joking. His was at the other end of the pits, newly constructed for three bikes, extra lighting, extra seats, goggle hooks etc. Obviously Ivan was Thommo's favourite son, I wonder why he is not writing this foreword, too expensive, maybe?

Ian Thomas is a one-off, that is for sure. We never had a contract at Hull, we didn't need it. He is a great promoter. He pays incredible attention to detail. Doesn't waste money, and is very strong on the accountancy side and always knows the break-even figure. He has an amazing feel of knowing what the speedway public wants. There is no one better in speedway to work with the media and gain the exposure and publicity that you need to be successful. In fact, Thommo is great for speedway.

As a Kiwi I would have to say he's really a good bloke.

IAN Thomas the speedway rider at Belle Vue.

1 - *Who is Ian Thomas?*

SO who is this Ian Thomas guy? If I had to sum myself up in a word I would choose 'entertainer'. That's what I have always tried to be in the best traditions of the famous old music halls and variety clubs of my home county, Yorkshire.

I guess I'm best known as one of Britain's longest-serving speedway promoters and the only man to manage England to the Grand Slam of World titles in 1980. I'm also the man who took the from the deserts of the Middle East, the ice rinks of Telford and the hallowed halls of Wembley Stadium.

It's all a far cry from when I saw my first speedway meeting at Bradford's Odsal Stadium in 1949 when I was seven and I've been hooked on the sport ever since. I used to go with a pair of goggles so I could stand as close as possible to the safety fence without getting my eyes filled with flying shale.

I'm also a professional magician with my own agency, which makes it easy for me to get bookings. Anything else? Well, I was useless at school, never passed an exam, got the sack from my first job and was a hopeless speedway rider. Pretty good, eh?

The only reason I became a promoter was because I knew I'd never make the grade as a rider and I had to stay in the sport. That's some CV but it has led me to a fantastic life where I've had huge success and massive failure, I've pulled a few stunts and a few deals and I've always tried to stay a step ahead of the field.

I've employed speedway legends like Barry Briggs and Ivan Mauger and I've rubbed shoulders with showbiz glitterati like Ken Dodd and Freddie Starr. I've got stories to tell about them all.

I love live entertainment. That's why I once worked as The Man in the Iron Mask with business partner and former rider Graham Drury as The Man with the Unrideable Bike. That's why I'll travel the length of Britain to watch Showaddywaddy or leave home 24 hours early for a speedway match at Eastbourne so I can take in a Vince Hill concert.

I love a show and I love to put one on for the people who pay at the door. They are the lifeblood of sport and showbusiness and they deserve the best I can give them, whether it's magic at a posh wedding or speedway on a filthy, freezing night in Manchester.

I've made money, lost the lot and made a comeback I'm entitled to be proud of. I've upset a few folk along the way and a few have rubbed me up the wrong way but I've had a fantastic life and I've met some marvellous and colourful people.

I was born in Ilkley on January 3, 1942 and I'm married to Dot after meeting her in the Mecca ballroom in Bradford. Our first date was to Belle Vue speedway, which she thought was brilliant because a lad normally took a girl to the cinema. Now we are coming up to our 40th anniversary and that means I could have murdered her four times and still be out of nick again! I've a son Lyndon, daughter-in-law Sara and granddaughter Mia.

I was thick at school, Otley Secondary Modern, and left at 15 when I wanted to be a police cadet. The careers officer told me that I wasn't tall enough and that I'd have to be 16 anyway to do that. So he got me a job as apprentice bricklayer. I went back to see him when I was 16 but I hadn't grown so I couldn't be a copper and that idea was knocked on the head.

I worked as a salesman for a wholesale clothing warehouse in Leeds and then took to the road as a rep. That was a great move because they gave me a vehicle. I put that to the primary use of transporting me and my speedway bike to training schools and anywhere I could get a race.

That was fine until I was supposed to be in Manchester selling ladies' clothing but I was, in fact, riding in the second half of a speedway meeting at Greenfield, Bradford. I survived the speedway but had an awful crash on the way home. The Fire Brigade had to cut my pal, Robin Wells, and me out of the car. The police told my dad we were both dead. Fortunately, like Mark Twain, rumours of our deaths had been greatly exaggerated.

But I wrote off the company car, which earned me the sack. I went on to be a rep for Beechams before selling mopeds for Raleigh Industries. I sold shirts on the side and did some wheeler-dealing. I had a partner, Jeff Brownhut, and we'd go down to the East End warehouses in London in a furniture van and buy anything we could get. Then we'd go round the fairgrounds and what we called the swag shops on the Yorkshire coast to sell the stuff. The swag shops were the ones that sold cheap souvenirs to holidaymakers while the fairgrounds used our stuff as prizes on the stalls.

It was quite good business but the fair people always paid in petty cash and I'd finish up with a bag full of pennies, sixpences (2.5p) and shillings (5p). I'd take it home and spend hours going through the lot with a coin book because some of them were worth more than their face value. It was arduous work and I never found anything worth a fortune but I reckoned to make a seven or eight per cent profit. It was hard graft going through all those coins but a profit is a profit.

The daftest buy I ever made was when my partner was ill. I went to London on my own and bought 5,000 bows for sixpence each. I thought it was a brilliant deal until I got back and Jeff asked me: "Where are the arrows?" I'd never thought of them. A bow without an arrow isn't much good at all but Jeff and I still managed to sell them

I'd always drop everything if anyone would give me ride in a speedway meeting. I rode at Belle Vue the week after Peter Craven was killed in 1963. I fell off when I was in third place – I didn't often get much higher than that – and there was another junior called John Jolly behind me. He was quite a way back so I thought I'd lie where I was to give him chance to miss me but he rode straight over me and I was carried off.

The only sport I was good at was cricket. I was an all-rounder and Somerset county player Johnny Lawrence, who lived in Rothwell, near Leeds, was my coach. He took me to Somerset for a trial and they offered me a contract as a junior professional. But I would have had to live down there and I wanted to be a speedway rider so I said no.

I was 27 when I started promoting speedway at Workington. Jeff was my partner because he'd got hooked when I took him to West Ham on one of our London trips. Since then, I've been at Hull, Barrow, Newcastle, Ellesmere Port and Belle Vue. At one time I ran four tracks at the same time by myself. Talk about stress.

I've been on the management committee of the British League's first division and vice chairman of the second division.

It has always been part of my business mantra that a deal is a deal. If it's agreed and sealed by a handshake, that's good enough for me. Barry Briggs and Ivan Mauger, two of the world's greatest riders, rode for me and neither of them had a written contract.

I even made a deal with myself 12 years ago and, to this day, I've kept it. I used to smoke an average of 55 cigarettes a day and stopped overnight after making a personal pact to pack in. My wife, Dot, said I could go to Thailand on my own if I did it but I haven't been yet.

The only time I came near to breaking the deal was when I went to a magic convention. I bought an illusion that I wanted to use at dinner shows when I went from table to table. It necessitated lighting a cigarette and then making it disappear. But I thought I could be lighting up ten cigarettes a night and that might get me in the habit again. It was a good illusion but I gave it away to another magician.

Well, that's me. This is my story. I want you to enjoy it. Is it a deal?

2 – The Comets take off

IT was 1970. I had been a speedway fan since 1949 and a total failure as a rider in the early 1960s before moving through an assortment of jobs and enterprises with Jeff Brownhut, my partner in a wholesale business. I had been desperate to stay in a sport I knew I would never grace as a rider and that dream became a reality when Jeff and I became the proud promoters of Workington speedway.

People often asked me after we opened: 'Why Workington?' My standard reply was: 'Why not?' It was certainly not nailed on as the venue at first because in 1969 we looked at a number of places in Cumberland, as it was known then before boundary changes led to it being called Cumbria.

We went to Brunton Park, the home of Carlisle United, but there was no chance of putting a track in there because the soccer pitch came up to the terracing and there was no room. Then we drove to the Recreation Ground, home of Whitehaven Rugby League. That was a laugh. We met the groundsman and told him what we wanted – a pitch with room to put a speedway track round the outside. He said that would be no problem because there was a footpath all the way round the stadium. We had a look inside the stadium but, like Carlisle, there just wasn't enough space.

We thanked him and headed up the coast to Derwent Park at Workington. I don't know if it was fate that the first two venues weren't suitable because the short drive from Whitehaven took us to the start of a remarkable chapter in the history of British speedway at one of its remotest outposts. We knew after one look at the Rugby League stadium that it had every chance with plenty of space round the pitch with the exception of what is now the back straight. We would need to take out six or seven rows of terracing to get the width of track we needed.

But we fancied it. Workington was what we were looking for and I went home to do some research about the Rugby League club. I discovered that they were struggling financially, the crowds were not good and the team was even worse. In fact, but for the continual injection of cash by the chairman, Tom Mitchell, there would have been no Rugby League in the town. There wouldn't have been a stadium, either, because he had built that as well. Mr. Mitchell, it soon emerged, was the man we had to get to know if we were to progress but, having said that, I had no idea at the time just how important he would be over a period of many years.

I came to have more respect for him than anyone else I have met in the rest of my life. It was ironic that when we were preparing to open Workington for the second time, 20 years later, he passed away. Wild horses wouldn't have kept me away from his funeral. He had been team manager of the Great Britain Rugby League team in 1958 and one of his dying wishes was that as many of the sport's legends as possible would be his pallbearers. Stars like Vince Karalius, Alex Murphy and Jim Mills were there along with Les and Peter Gourlay and a local guy called Alan Varty. But I digress.

I soon discovered that you didn't have meetings with Mr. Mitchell – it was years before I called him Tom. I arranged an audience with him for Jeff and myself at his home. It was a very hot day so we parked just short of his house to put on our ties and jackets and generally smarten ourselves up before knocking on his door. We were greeted by Mrs. Mitchell, a charming lady, who escorted us through the house into the garden. I remember it as if it was yesterday. He was sitting on a chair wearing an Australian bush hat, a pair of sunglasses and a pair of shorts. He was reading The Times newspaper. He peered at us over his glasses and said: 'Good afternoon, take a seat.' That was very sociable apart from the fact there no chairs. He meant on the grass so down we went – psychological victory No. 1 for Mr. Mitchell who sat there looking down at us.

We outlined our plans, he asked what seemed like three million questions and then asked us to meet him at Derwent Park two hours later. He wasn't happy about us needing to remove the terracing but I said that while I could understand his reluctance, they were hardly packing the place. Finally, we agreed a rental of £100 per meeting. I asked him about planning permission and he said I wasn't to worry about that. He just told us to start work, which we did. We got our licence from the British Promoters' Association and didn't have too much spare cash when we started work on the track.

We arranged it so that most of the bills would not be due until after the first meeting. If that match had gone wrong, we would have been in trouble. It was that tight. We employed the late Vic Lonsdale, a rider who was known as the Wild Man, to be in charge of the track work and he also became our first captain. Vic was a character – I once booked him to ride at Long Eaton and he turned up at Nuneaton! We paid him a fixed sum per week for the contract and, out of that, he had to supply his own workmen. I noticed there never seemed to be any staff there on a Thursday morning and I later discovered why. It was dole day in Workington so we can only assume where Vic found his work force.

We were grafting one morning when an officious council official turned up and said: 'Stop work at once. You don't have planning permission.' I told the lads to down tools and phoned Mr. Mitchell to tell him of the problem. He soon arrived, looked at the redundant gang, and said: 'Start them up again and don't take notice of anyone but me.' I said: 'Okay Mr. Mitchell.' We resumed and never heard another thing. We never saw any more officious officials, either. It transpired that we never did have planning permission to run speedway at Derwent Park and that fact was confirmed when we dug out the archives for Tony Mole, who took over the licence in 1999.

The next job, after Vic and his crew had finished the track, was to build a team. Reg Wilson and Bob Valentine came on loan from Sheffield, Taffy Owen was signed from Rochdale, Vic himself agreed a deal and I brought in Aussies Chris Blythe and Mal Mackay as well as Lou Sansom, who became the darling of the Comets' fans in that era. Lou was due to travel over with Jimmy Gavros, brother of Halifax rider Dennis, but, tragically, he was killed just before he was due to leave. London-based Geoff Penniket also joined us.

I can claim to have taken two sporting legends to Cumbria in the two spells I have been there. Sansom was the first and Carl Stonehewer remains the second Derwent Park hero. I signed Lou through my friendship with Dennis Gavros, who lived in the same city, Adelaide. He stayed with Dennis in Halifax for the first couple of years in England before moving up to Workington and subsequently marrying a local girl.

Lou's popularity stemmed from his looks and the fact that he was immaculate on and off the track. He modelled himself on Ivan Mauger and even had the same black and white chess board checks on his gear. He bought gear from Ivan and, also like the great man, he could be sharp away from the starts.

One year I failed to agree deals with Lou and Taffy Owen and started the season without them. It was big news because they were both fan heroes so I got on the microphone at the first match and explained that, if I caved in to their pay demands, I would have to increase the cost of admission by 25p per person per meeting. I said I wasn't prepared to do that for two riders and got almost a standing ovation. They were there ready to race the following week at the rate they had been offered.

Wheels and Deals

When Lou was staying in Halifax both he and I had to travel home along the A65 from near Kendal to Skipton. One night, in the early hours, I came up behind him where the road runs parallel with the railway line at Settle. He appeared to be parked rather dangerously on a narrow piece of road so, fearing there was a problem, I stopped behind him and went to see why he was sitting there. 'The lights have been on red for ages,' he explained. I looked up. He was waiting for a railway signal to change!

Workington rolled into action on April 3, 1970 when Berwick were the visitors in the Border Trophy, a meeting we lost by one point. Entrance prices were two shillings and sixpence (12.5 new pence), 3s 6d (17.5 new pence) and 4s 6d (22.5 new pence). Programmes were sixpence (2.5 new pence). The official pay rate was 50p a start and 50p a point but I doubled that for most of the team and was regarded as a good payer.

Reg Wilson, who we billed as the Blond Bombshell, came up to me one night and said: 'Excuse me, Mr. Thomas, but will this track ever be smooth?' I said: 'I don't think so.' Reg replied: 'Okay.' And went back to his bike. Reg got me in deep trouble with the Workington faithful when I opened at Hull in 1971. He told me he wanted to ride there instead because the trip north was too far. It took the fans a long time to forgive me for that and it is still mentioned to this day. But it wasn't my fault.

We opened to a crowd of more than 8,000, which was fabulous. The trouble was that only 6,000 paid and I make no apology for repeating this story, which has gone round the speedway world. The non-payers really bugged me. I, and others, had put in a lot of work while Jeff and I had invested virtually all our money. We needed that gate revenue to pay waiting bills and I discovered that people had gained free admission by crawling over a pipe that crossed the river at a point where there was no perimeter fence. Get over the pipe and you were in, but only for that week. Anyone who tried it the next week was in all right – in the river! I put a load of grease on the pipe and anyone who tried it again got a soaking. They fell in like flies. What a shame! I once had a Czech fan arrive for a meeting and he asked to see the famous pipe because he had read about it back home. But, sadly, that little bit of speedway folklore had been removed by then. Even so, we were open and, at last, I was a speedway promoter. Boy, was I happy about that.

The first away match for the Comets was a league fixture at Rochdale and that provided another rare, if not unique, incident.

Chris Blythe and Mal Mackay were our riders in one heat that was stopped by an almighty pile-up on the first bend. It was carnage with all four on the deck. The referee, the late Jack Ashworth, excluded both Rochdale riders and I was left with a broad grin in anticipation of a 5-0 advantage in the re-run. I told my guys not to do anything daft and they duly completed the race without incident. But my grin was soon wiped away when referee Ashworth then disqualified them for not making a bona-fide effort to race. I went nuts. You don't get many nil-nil heat results in speedway.

The Derwent Park track record in that first meeting was set at 83 seconds by Berwick's Andy Meldrum but it shows just how much quicker the sport is now because Simon Stead has clocked 64.1. It's a massive difference because, basically, the track is the same. Simon, in fact, could do four laps while Andy did three at that rate. The Rugby League club had the catering rights and used to order – and sell – 1,200 pies per meeting. That's more pies than some clubs get fans these days.

Mr. Mitchell became a supporter and his favourite rider was Taffy Owen. When Taffy came into the bar after a meeting he would have a gin and tonic waiting for him. If he had done well, Mr. Mitchell would put a £10 note in his top pocket. I remember one night when Taffy flew head first over the safety fence. What a wallop. He looked to be in a sorry state and was taken to hospital where they wanted to detain him overnight for observation. But Taffy discharged himself and, to everyone's amazement, turned up in the bar. I said: 'What are you doing here?' He replied: 'I wanted my gin and tonic and £10 from Mr. Mitchell.'

I brought a lot of attractions to Workington over the years and one that was completely speedway orientated was a series of match races between Kiwi legends Barry Briggs and Ivan Mauger. It was exhibition, really, but they pulled in a crowd and what an exhibition they gave. In the third race, with Ivan on the inside, they raced shoulder to shoulder for four laps and, on each corner, Briggo had his left foot resting on Ivan's bike. It was clever stuff. Brilliant.

The Rugby League club became my partners after a couple of years when Jeff Brownhut sold his shares to them and, at last, I was allowed to call Mr. Mitchell by his Christian name, Tom. George Graham, one of the directors, looked after the club's speedway interests and, for a short while, he was involved in Newcastle and Barrow speedway with me.

I wanted to run a stunt show at the stadium and asked Tom if I could rent it. He said it wouldn't attract a crowd and that I'd lose a lot of money. I told him, with all due respect, that was my problem and he gave me the use of the stadium rent free. The show, which he attended in his big hat, attracted more than 8,000 people and I was off to the bank with a smile on my face. I had an appointment with Tom at his home the next day. We had one thing in common – we were both very stubborn people. He hated to admit he was wrong but I went in, thanked him for the use of the stadium and said I would pay double the speedway rental if he said I was right. He looked over his glasses at me and growled: 'You were right.' I duly gave him £200 and he poured me a glass of his finest port. I had so much respect for the man and nobody who has followed him at Derwent Park could lick his boots.

He was a fascinating character who owned a slice of Workington town as well as a castle in Malta, a theatre in Edinburgh and he worked for the Government. He would never say what his job was but I think he was a spy. He travelled the world's trouble spots and I have been in his presence when Margaret Thatcher phoned him – at least that's what he told me. His son, Ian, still came down as a supporter during my second spell at the club.

I'll be eternally grateful to Tom Mitchell, Workington speedway, and the Cumbrian supporters for the part they have played in my story. I must also put on record my appreciation of the support given by the late Eric Easterbrook, who gave us terrific coverage in the News and Star, the local evening paper.

We had to use a lot of Australian riders because the club's geographical position meant that many home riders were put off by the time it took to get up there, even though it was such a scenic run. Workington was a lively place after meetings in those days with the boys and girls partying all over town. We were asked to leave most of the town's hotels at some time or other.

A promoter shouldn't have favourites in his team but I have to confess I did at Derwent Park. He was Steve Watson, a local lad, who still watches the Comets most weeks. He was an average second string who once held the record for the most consecutive appearances for the club. Steve was in seventh or eighth heaven riding for his hometown team and he is responsible for my all-time favourite story, one that I always include in an after-dinner speech or talk.

Steve was totally blind in one eye and, because of that, he wouldn't be permitted to ride in this day and age but he was then. One Friday night at Derwent Park he had the most dreadful crash, piling head first into the safety fence on the third bend. The pits are on the first bend so I set off running across the centre green. Steve was laid out and I genuinely feared the worst. He started to come round as I got to him and I asked him: 'How are you?' His reply was the best one liner I have ever heard: 'I'm okay. I've got double vision for the first time in my life.' A classic.

The crowds started dropping after four years at Workington and I began sniffing around for another track. The opportunity to open at Newcastle became a possibility and, after one more season, I sold my shares to the Rugby League club. I opened in the North East in 1975, little knowing that 25 years later I would be be back at Workington as team manager and co-promoter with Tony Mole.

I learned a lot at Derwent Park and it gave me a great grounding in being a speedway boss. I discovered there were some very good and clever promoters in the sport. I also learned there were a few who could run a speedway club okay – and a few more who couldn't run a bath!

COMEDIAN Ken Dodd with Ian Thomas.

3 – Characters: four of the best

I'VE booked many interval and pre-match attractions at speedway over the years. It's part of my desire to be an entertainer and to put on as good a show as I mentioned in the introduction. One thing I've never done is increase the cost of admission to a meeting to cover the extra expense. Fans pay at the gate to see a speedway meeting and, if I want to give them something extra, it's up to me. It also means nobody can complain about being charged extra to see someone they don't like.

I had an unforgettable night when I booked the one and only Ken Dodd to appear at Workington. It would be fair to say that Doddy didn't do many gigs in Workington but I know that he has never forgotten this one. I think the same goes for the people who were at Derwent Park that night – and a few more who weren't!

Ken Dodd was special, unique. He was a megastar then in the world of comedy and still is. Without question, he put more bums on seats that any one rider ever did. I booked him for October 27, 1972 when the grandstand held 1,100 people. I decided to make it all-ticket and let the public pre-book their seats week by week.

I booked him for the end-of-season meeting, which I called the Ken Dodd Trophy, but we got so many column inches that I put the tickets up for sale a week earlier than planned and sold out in four days. That was four weeks before he was due to appear and was good business by anyone's standards.

Ken is famed for the length of time he spends on stage when he's doing a show. He regards them as parties and says who wants a good party to stop? But I also knew through my showbusiness experience that when he was doing a personal appearance, as against a theatre booking, he always arrived late. The last thing I wanted for a 7.30 start at Workington was Ken Dodd arriving at 8.30 and missing the pre-meeting parade. So I booked him for 6.30 and he turned up at 7.15 – and that was still cutting it close enough to worry my chuckle bone.

I took the opportunity to ask him why he had built up this reputation for lateness when he was always on time for his stage shows and the answer was that of the real old pro he is. He said: 'A crowd builds a crowd. If I'm booked to open a supermarket at 7.00pm there will only be a few people there at that time. But once a few people gather, more keep coming to see what's happening.'

It was the same as if you stood on your own in the middle of

Wheels and Deals

Manchester and looked up. Before long you would be surrounded by people wanting to see what you were looking at. Doddy used the same principle to build a crowd. He could do it without even being there.

My deal with Ken was that I'd pay him a fee and it was also agreed he could sell his Diddymen toys. He brought a lot with him and sold out. In return he would judge an interval competition for kids dressed up as Diddymen with prizes for the best three. It was absolutely wonderful to watch him in action and there's no doubt that he enjoyed it as much as the kids.

I'd also booked an organist who was wired through to the centre green so Doddy could have live backing to sing a few songs, tell a few gags and then we could get on with the second half of the meeting. Or so I planned. I should have known better. There never was a second half that night.

The Ken Dodd Trophy was completed by the interval and Crewe star John Jackson won it. Re-enter Doddy. He made the presentations without any problems. Then he was confronted by 40 or 50 real life Diddymen when the kids came out. He wasn't going to miss a chance like that and he didn't. He got them on the track and took off with them all following him. He looked like the Pied Piper. The kids were dancing away behind him, having a ball, while Doddy told jokes on the radio microphone as he went round.

It was an unbelievable sight. He finally chose the three winners of the competition, the kids went back into the crowd, the organist struck up and he stood out there for more than an hour singing and telling jokes. There was no time left for the second half, which was cancelled, but nobody minded and nobody left the stadium until he'd finished a brilliant night.

He'd done a full night for us so I asked him if he fancied a bite to eat if I could find somewhere still serving meals at around 11 o'clock. He said yes. It wasn't easy finding somewhere in Workington at that time of night but the name Ken Dodd might have helped and the Brierli House Hotel said they would sort something out for us. It's still there on the road out of Workington.

When we arrived they ushered us into the restaurant, which was shut, and we had a choice of roast pork or roast pork. So we had roast pork. The bar was open in another part of the hotel but the word got out that Doddy was around and people started coming in for autographs while we were waiting for the meal. He signed them happily enough but, just as the food arrived, he stood up, went into the bar and did a 20-minute spot.

I asked his driver why he was doing that when he'd worked all night and wasn't getting paid for doing it. He said it was because he realised they were the people who paid his wages. He came back and ate a cold dinner.

Not many people know this but Doddy is a big fan of magicians which is why he often has one on his shows. As as you may know by now, I also work in that line and every February I attend the world's biggest magic convention in Blackpool. There are around 3,000 magicians in attendance and dealers from all over the world turn up. Doddy blocks off a day in his diary to go and every time I've bumped into him there he always says: 'How's Workington speedway?' It's probably the only speedway track he's been to but that's after more than 30 years and that's the measure of a true star. He's magic.

One of my more recent bookings is Ove Fundin, one of speedway's real legends. Everything about his brilliant career, which includes five World titles, must have been written 100 times. He lives with his Romanian wife, Ioana, on a golf course in the south of France where he plays almost every day.

I've had the pleasure of playing with him on several occasions and won the Rider Cup with him. I just love the name. It's a competition run by the Veterans' Association but how many people can say they've won the Rider Cup? I can!

Several years ago I joined Ove, Speedway Star proprietor Phil Rising and Editor Richard Clark (caddie) for a round at a small course in Sweden before a Grand Prix. We had a leisurely lunch in the clubhouse afterwards and it was fascinating to sit back and listen to the great man.

It would seem he is a person to whom no challenge is too great. He told us how he had cycled from his home in France to his home country of Sweden, camping along the way. I couldn't believe anyone would do that, especially when they could just hop on a plane. I asked him why and he said as if it was the reason anyone would do such a thing: 'I wanted to see how long it would take me.' There was no answer to that.

He then asked me a question and it's one I wished I could have answered. He looked back to the golden days of speedway when he was winning World titles in a packed Wembley stadium and said: "What did the British promoters do with the 75,000 half-crowns (12.5p) that came through the turnstiles all those years? Was it not foolish in that era that they didn't re-invest in the future of the sport?"

I remember saying to Richard Clark after lunch that someone

should get Ove's story down in a book for posterity and I understand that is now happening. Put me down for a copy.

When I was planning the opening meeting at Belle Vue in 2005, after Tony Mole had taken over, I wanted the club's former World Champions Ove, Ivan Mauger and Peter Collins to be there along with Jason Crump, then the current champion, who was riding on the night. We started with the Peter Craven Memorial Trophy in respect to the club's late double World Champion and were delighted that his widow Brenda, now Mrs Leat, was able to join us.

When I asked Ove to come he just said 'Sure.' That was it. No questions. He is part of the history of Belle Vue in particular and speedway in general and goodness knows how many autographs he signed that night but it must have run into four figures. He never refused one. I couldn't help wondering if some modern sportsmen, who will never aspire to his kind of success, would have done it.

Ove is a legend and a gentleman.

I've already mentioned my third character in passing in this chapter. That's Speedway Star editor, Richard Clark. I've known him since he was a rookie in the business and he'll never forget the first time he made a foreign trip with me. He's made hundreds over the years but never one quite like this.

Clarkie tells me that the first time we met was in a hotel in Gothenburg where I found myself staying along with the Press lads for the 1980 World Final which was won by Michael Lee as part of my Grand Slam year. Most of the national papers sent reporters in those days and I was holding court as England manager into the early hours.

It was around 2am when I said that I was going to bed when I'd finished my drink. The next time I looked at my watch it was 5am and I was still there. Apparently the late Gordon Burnett, from the Daily Express, had been topping up my drink all night so I never did finish it.

That was my first real encounter with Clarkie and the next was when Graham Drury and I were taking a party of young riders to do an indoor meeting in Germany. I asked Richard if he fancied the trip and he accepted. More fool him! We picked him up en route in the van on the way to Dover and, just before we arrived there, he asked for his ferry ticket.

I told him it was a low budget trip and there wasn't one. I told him he'd have to hide under the mattress in the back of the van and, once we were at sea, he could come out. He gave me a look and said: "Are you serious?" I said: "I've never been more serious in my life." He said: "How about coming back?" I said: "Just the same."

So, to be fair to him, he got under the mattress and away we went. The van started to play up en route to Germany but we finally arrived and, while the riders went to practise, Clarkie and myself decided to go for a meal. We went to an Aberdeen Angus steak house and I decided to wind him up. That's easy. All I had to do was to tell him what a good Prime Minister Margaret Thatcher was and away he went with enough conversation for two courses. He also hates the pre-match and interval attractions that I put on at speedway meetings. He can't understand why I do it so that saw us through another course.

The meeting was okay but we were still facing the problem of a dodgy van for the trip home. Being the true professional he is, Richard was worried about getting back in time for the Speedway Star Press day. He didn't want to risk missing the deadline so he asked me if I would lend him a few pounds so he could fly back, which I did. It also saved him from getting under the mattress again! And he did pay me back.

To Clarkie's credit, it didn't stop him joining Graham and myself on a trip to Northern Ireland where we were putting on an ice meeting at Dundonald, near Belfast. The riders, referee John Whittaker and Richard followed the day after us – he had a 'plane ticket this time. We were staying in Bangor on the coast but Clarkie was desperate to go into a well-known Guinness bar, the Crown Liquor Saloon, in Belfast.

The troubles were at the height at the time and there were armed soldiers on the streets. I wasn't happy about going into Belfast with him because he had a huge black beard at the time and looked like a terrorist. I thought there was no way we wouldn't get pulled by the security forces if we tried to drive into Belfast at night.

But he was insistent. He had to go so we decided to give it a try. We drove straight through the first road block but we weren't so lucky at the second. A rifle came through the car window with a soldier behind it and he asked where we were going. I told him we were promoting ice speedway meetings and that we were heading for the famous Guinness bar. Then he said: "Who's that in the back with the beard?" I said: "You had better ask him."

So they got Clarkie out, he talked his way through it and off we went for a drink. That, I thought, was it. But he was in an adventurous mood and, perhaps, he was in the mood for revenge for the mattress incident. He said he wanted to drive up the Falls Road and down the Shankill Road, the two thoroughfares above all others that you avoid in Belfast.

Wheels and Deals

I'd done it on a previous trip but I said: "That's pushing it a bit." We were all very wary of the situation but we went. I drove up the Falls Road and it was fascinating with all the stuff painted on the walls and the security. We'd shoved Clarkie in the back seat and the last thing I intended to do was to stop. We got to the top in the pitch black and were just going to hook a left into Shankill Road when he decided he wants to spend a penny.

I said: "There aren't a lot of public toilets at the top of the Falls Road, Clarkie." He said: "I'm bursting." There was an abandoned garage so I stopped, told him to get out and to be quick. Very quick. Hardly had he got started when there was a noise above and an Army helicopter came over. They put a searchlight on him and I yelled: "Get back in here before we get shot." He rushed back and, fortunately, we got back in one piece.

I've always regarded him as being more than a good speedway writer. He's also what I'd call an observation journalist and he's written some wonderful articles about Workington. You can trust him implicitly with an off-the-record story and you can't pay a journalist a bigger compliment than that.

The final character I want to recall has nothing whatsoever to do with speedway but it is a story that no-one could make up. It's stranger than fiction. Over the years I've taken 17 productions out to the Middle East, either speedway, ice shows or magic. One of them was Aladdin on Ice. We went for 20 days to do 48 shows and I was the compere as well as the organiser. I never want to hear, read or see anything about Aladdin ever again.

I had been asked by a contact out there to set up the show in a country which I won't name. The reason will become clear. I hadn't a clue how to organise an ice show but, like I always do, I said 'Yes' and worried about how I'd do it afterwards. I was given a budget and went to Toys 'R Us to buy a book about Aladdin. I had about ten weeks to get it organised so I circulated the British ice dancing world about what I was doing.

I booked a pair of former World ice dance champions to top the bill and sub-contracted the hiring of the rest of the skaters to them. I booked an ice rink in Wales to rehearse the show. The cast numbered 15 with the World champions, a stunt skater and a chorus line of young, attractive female skaters. The opening night was attended by members of the local Royal Family. We were about 25 minutes into the show and the stunt dancer, a really talented lad from Blackpool, was hurtling up to a ramp to do a big somersault when all the lights went out. It was prayer time but my only prayers were for this lad who had suddenly found himself flying through the air in the dark. The lights came back on and, fortunately, he had landed safely and was just sitting there on the ice looking bemused.

But I digress. After the shows we would go from hotel to hotel for a drink. In one of them I met an Arab who was one of the biggest men I have ever met. He must have been nearly seven feet tall. He was built like one of those huge trucks you see in American road movies. That's why I called him Diesel because I never discovered his real name, even though we became really friendly over a short period of time. He was a really nice guy.

I never asked him what he did for a living and he never told me. One night I was in this particular hotel watching a brilliant Filipino band and several of our dancers were there, too. They were obviously very fit as well as being very tidy and were a massive hit with the Arab guys. It didn't surprise me because I'd had the experience on an earlier trip when an Omani guy had offered me two camels for my wife, Dot. I told him she was worth at least three but he wouldn't go to that!

Two of the dancers in particular were being pestered by a couple of these Arabs who wouldn't take no for an answer. They asked me to tell them to back off and leave them alone which I did, three times, without succcess. We were in a two-tiered bar and the girls were in one section while I was in the other with Diesel. Finally, I told him that I'd got a problem with the two Arabs and would he be in a position to help me.

He said: "Follow me, Ian." I did. He went through to the other bar, went up to the Arabs and spoke to them in Arabic. They looked absolutely terrified. He picked up one in each hand by the scruff of the neck. He told me to open the door which I did. He carried them up a flight of stairs and told me to open another door which I did. He never said a word but just threw them out into the street. They didn't come back, we went back to our seats in the bar and the girls never had any more problems.

The next day I was talking to some government officials and I mentioned the incident with the guy I called Diesel. They told me why the girls didn't have any more problems.

Diesel worked for the government, doing a month on duty and a month off. He was on duty… which is why he was staying at the hotel. His job? He was the state executioner.

4 – Life at the Boulevard

I OPENED speedway in Hull 1971 and closed it ten eventful years later. But I can reveal now that a wheel should never have been permitted to turn at The Boulevard.

In the first place, Hull speedway almost never happened because it wasn't easy obtaining planning permission to run. Along with Exeter, it was situated in the most populated area of any track in the United Kingdom but it was finally granted and, when we opened, I had 60 per cent of the stake in the club with co-promoter Wally Mawdsley holding the other 40 per cent.

Colin Tucker, from New Zealand, built and maintained the track and, while he was there, most riders recognised it as the best surface in speedway. But the truth of the matter is that the track shouldn't have been put down in the first place because there wasn't enough room for the straights. In reality, it wasn't possible to have a minimum sized Rugby League pitch with a speedway track outside it but I was determined that such a technicality wasn't going to stop me.

The minimum width of a straight should have been 25 feet but we only had room for 24, even with the rugby pitch left as small as it could go. What helped was the fact that I had my own tape measure with the first foot cut off because that eased the problem a bit. The initial track inspection to decide whether or not we could race on the new circuit was conducted by the Speedway Control Board's Bill Kitchen, the former England and Wembley star. He was a lovely man who liked to reminisce about the old days.

When it came to the part of the inspection where everything had to be measured, Bill said he would have to nip back to his car for his tape. I told him not to bother because I just happened to have one in my pocket so we used my special tape instead. I started talking about the old days and the old riders to try to distract him a bit while we did the business. I held the end of the tape that was a bit on the short side. He was on the other end adding it up and he said that we'd just made it. We passed the rest of the inspection with flying colours and Hull were in business.

I left The Boulevard ten years later during which time, as I will relate, I took two of the sport's legends to Humberside in Barry Briggs and Ivan Mauger, as well as the Moran brothers, who became legends in their own rather different ways.

Wheels and Deals

But I had to live with the secret knowledge that we could have been closed down at any time. John Berry, the former Ipswich promoter, mentions an instance in his book when he and his team manager, Ron Bagley, went over to the back straight on the far side of the track from the main stand during a meeting armed with a tape measure. They were obviously suspicious about the width and he was trying to be smart but he wasn't smart enough because I jumped in and asked two police officers to escort them off the centre green.

More than 7,000 people came in for the opening night. They were coming from all directions and I'm pretty sure that not all of them paid. I've still got a cine film clip showing my former secretary, Lesley, standing by the stadium wall with a big stick. She was hitting any hands that appeared on the top of the wall to repel any would-be spectators who were trying to climb over for a free view. If she saw a hand, she hit it. No promoter likes people to sneak in without paying but the real time to worry is when they don't even want to watch the racing for nothing.

The Hull Press Officer at that time was my old friend, Richard Bott, who wrote the programme and did the Press releases. He still does the job for me at the annual Telford ice meeting. We pulled off some great stunts to launch a new season and it was a vibrant scene for many years. It was always lively in the bar after a meeting and it was a fair bet that there would be a few invitations flying round to go on to a party. Dick and I accepted one such invite to go on for a few drinks after we'd had a good win. On arrival, it was full of fans and we were led up into a big loft where we were given a drink.

We had been there for about 15 minutes when I started to smell something and it certainly wasn't methanol. I looked at Dick and he asked if I could smell something the same as him. I said yes. This was at a time when speedway got good coverage in the National Press and they would just love a sleaze story. Dick said: "Can you imagine the column inches we would get if the Hull promoter and a Daily Express sports writer were caught in a drugs den?" In true newspaper style, we made our excuses and left.

One night, about ten minutes before the start of a big meeting, I received a call from a high-ranking police officer to tell me they had been given a bomb warning. I asked him what I should do and not only did his answer amaze me, but it happened again at a later date. He said the decision was mine. I had around 3,750 people in the stadium so it was going to be a good pay night. Dick was in the office with me and he asked me what I was going to do. I said I was going to run the meeting – and watch it from the centre spot of the rugby pitch. He asked if he could come out there with me and I said 'Certainly.' Needless to say, there was no bomb.

I have already mentioned that speedway attracted good coverage in the National Press in those days and we got a tip that the News of the World were sending an undercover team to a meeting in search of a sleaze story. I warned the riders of both teams that it was in their interest to stay out of the bar after the meeting and avoid the risk of being caught in any sort of compromising position. I suggested they got a shower and hit the road home which they did. In order to remain anonymous the reporters had paid to get in, which pleased me of course. But I sussed out one of them because I was told he had been asking questions and, at the end of the night, I walked up to him and said: 'You've got bugger all, have you?'

I've always had a great relationship with the media and I'm proud of the friendships I've formed with many of the Press lads over the years. I know the value of publicity and if they want stories, I'll always find one for them. But I could never tolerate the kind of journalist who came to The Boulevard that night with the only intention of digging dirt. In my view they come into the low life bracket.

Hull were in the Second Division when I opened there and, overall, they were good times. That didn't include the night Tony Childs, who rode for me for a spell, jumped on the bonnet of my Rolls Royce at Boston and didn't do it much good. I can't recall why he did it. I didn't find him a particularly nice person but he was a character.

One of the big events in Hull every year was the town fair. It was massive, almost as big as the Nottingham Goose Fair. One of the attractions was a Wall of Death ride and I contacted the owner to ask if one my team could have a go. He agreed because it was good publicity for both of us. Then it was a matter of finding someone daft enough to do it and, because he was a bit of a nutter, I persuaded Tony to tackle the job. He was great, the media turned out in force and we all got massive coverage.

I ran Second Division speedway at Hull for three seasons and then bought Coatbridge's First Division licence and moved up into the big league in 1974 with a new-look team but the same old track that wasn't wide enough. The team had to be strengthened and I also purchased two of the Coatbridge assets, Jimmy McMillan and Bobby Beaton, who turned out to be wonderful acquisitions.

I have written elsewhere in the book about some of the big names who I signed for Hull and another was the German longtrack superstar and pop singer, Egon Muller. He was an incredibly charismatic bloke who only did a limited amount of speedway but he managed to qualify for the 1976 World Final at Wembley. Barry Briggs, who was based in Germany while riding for Hull, was competing with Muller on a regular basis on the Continent and, halfway through the season, he asked me if I fancied bringing him into British speedway. You can imagine my reaction when I had a rider like Muller virtually handed to me on a plate.

Egon was keen to come over, admittedly for a limited spell, to sharpen up his speedway skills on UK tracks ahead of Wembley. Briggo, who was already staying at my house on the edge of Ilkley Moor, said Muller could travel with him and I said I could accommodate the pair of them. So he signed for Hull but what I paid him has never been revealed. He was a multi World longtrack champion and a megastar in Europe but he agreed to ride for the princely fee of £50 a meeting – and he paid his own air fares. I told him that we could give him the chance he wanted to ride over here but that I was over budget and couldn't afford a major deal. He was riding for us at a loss but we were doing him a favour.

He put 1,000 extra people on the gate on the night of his debut. The only problem was that he didn't turn up and, to this day, I don't know why. That wasn't my prime concern when I looked out at all the extra punters who had come to see someone who wasn't there. I know the value of good publicity but I also knew the damage that could be caused by a bad Press and I had to do something urgently. I took the bull by the horns, went out onto the centre green on the mike to make a public apology and said that anyone who wanted to leave before the meeting could have their admission money refunded. I didn't want to con anyone but only about eight people took up the offer with the rest staying. I also booked him once for the indoor speedway show at Wembley Arena. He turned up, said he couldn't ride because of an injury but said he'd go out and sing for us instead at half price.

Muller only rode eight league matches for us and they included a round trip for meetings against Newport at the old Somerton Park track and Cradley Heath the next night. The boys were booked into a hotel at Newport and Frank Auffret was rooming with Egon who I needed to talk to. I knocked on the door, went in and there was what I took to be girl sitting there blow waving a head full of blond hair. I apologised and went to shut the door but realised that it was Egon. Frank was lying on his bed out of sight laughing his head off. Most riders prepare for a meeting by checking their bikes or having a rest. Egon did his hair.

He had a pile-up late in the meeting with a Newport rider who was excluded. Egon was stretched out on the track doing a dying swan act but we desperately needed him to go out for the re-run. Rules prevented us from replacing him and we needed the point he would get for third place to win the match. He didn't want to do it but a couple of the boys sorted out his bike while Briggo and myself got him back to the pits. We promised sarcastically to get him to hospital for multiple X-rays on his little finger if first he would just tootle round for the crucial point. He said it would be very dangerous but went out and we won the match. The next match at Cradley turned out to be his last for us but it was fun while it lasted.

I have good memories of Egon racing for Hull but my fondest recollection has nothing to do with speedway. One of the days he stayed with us he was in the garden with my son, Lyndon, who was only a nipper at the time, and Egon amazed him by picking up a bee from a flower. He could hold it in his hand and it would never sting him. Obviously he told Lyndon not to try it, and I'll say the same to anyone reading this, but I've no idea how he could do it. It certainly wasn't my brand of magic. I'd be fascinated to know how he found out he could do it.

I will have to be careful how I tell this story but one year during my time at Hull, Reading promoter Reg Fearman attracted some good pre-season publicity when he took out his team, with their girlfriends and wives, for a champagne dinner. It was a good bonding exercise and I decided to do something similar but different. Very different as it turned out!

I took the team to the Dragonara Hotel and Casino, in Leeds, which is now the Hilton. We used to call in there on the way home from Hull meetings for a gamble and also because they provided punters with free sandwiches and drinks. So I took the team to the casino and then it was off to a massage and sauna parlour in the city where the club paid for the services rendered. It also explains why I can't say which year it was! When one of the lads came out of a massage room, another went in and was heard to say: 'I don't know what he had but I'll have the same.'

In all the years I was at Hull, the only trophy we won was the Inter League Cup but we had a lot of big meetings and they included a Test match between England and Australia which was sponsored by Durex. They used one of our rooms as a hospitality suite to entertain their guests and the riders after the meeting. Samples of their products were placed round the room in bowls and some had been taken before the lads came in. But there were still loads left when the riders came in until one, who must remain nameless, went round the bowls and nicked the lot. I never knew he was that fit but it must have taken him months to use them.

Speedway isn't all fun because of the ever-present danger factor and one of the worst nights that I'll never forget was when Joe Owen had an horrendous crash on the second bend at Hull. He went bodily through the wooden safety fence. I went along to hospital with his family and we were told by our track doctor, Dr. Scott, that he was in a very serious condition in the operating theatre. Joe had suffered multiple injuries and we were informed that the surgeons didn't expect him to survive.

He was in the theatre through the early hours and Dr. Scott kept us informed all the way through. It was still touch and go after the operation when Joe was taken to the intensive care unit. It was a desperately anxious time for everyone, especially his family. I was allowed in to see him the next day and he seemed to have pipes coming out of everywhere, but he made a complete recovery and came back to speedway just as good a rider as ever. Sadly, however, the fates hadn't finished with Joe because later in his career, when he was riding for Ellesmere Port in 1985, he suffered terrible injuries at Birmingham which resulted in him being paralysed from the waist down.

I was very close to Joe and felt I knew him well because he had ridden for me for several years at Newcastle and Hull. I didn't think he would be able to cope mentally with being paralysed but he has adapated extremely well. I don't see him too often these days but we met at Barry Briggs' 70th birthday bash and he was very well and happy. He has built a new life for himself and I am delighted about that.

Brian Larner had joined the promotion and we had a lot of good years together at The Boulevard before our acrimonious split at Newcastle in 1984. When we first went in there, the Rugby League club were struggling and, at times, we paid them our rent in advance so they could pay their players. In the later years, there was a Rugby League boom and they were the ones getting the big crowds. Suddenly, we became a nuisance to them and they terminated our contract on the basis that we hadn't cleaned the stadium properly. How can you define cleaning a stadium properly?

We took legal advice over the matter but the cost of taking them to court would have been astronomical and we had to let it go. Hull closed in 1981 and, while it's a long time ago now, I still feel that there were people at the Rugby League club with very short memories. They were happy enough to take our money when they were in trouble.

However, I'd prefer to end my Hull memories with a smile rather than a grimace. It's a story involving that grand lad, Frank Auffret. I used to have greyhounds running at Leeds and people used to ask me why I bothered when I was so busy with speedway. The answer, dare I say, was that my wife, Dot, used to complain that we didn't go out often enough for a meal. So I bought the dogs and we used to eat at the track.

For publicity purposes, I called one dog Speedway Champ and the other Speedway Rider. He wasn't a very good dog because he kept getting disqualified for fighting but he won a race or two. Champ was a cracker and she won 18 good class races. Then she broke a hock and I was advised that she wouldn't run again so I should have her put down. I refused to do that and she did come back to win a few more races before the end of her career when I was told to consider letting her turn to breeding.

I paid a lot of money to have her covered by a top class dog in the Midlands and she had seven pups. To cut a long story short, none of them would race. I wouldn't have them put down so I found homes for them and Frank, who had a smallholding, said he'd like one. He put it in the back of his car and took it home with him to Middlesbrough.

He called me the next day and said: "You know that dog you gave me? It messed in the car all the way home and, when I woke up this morning, it had killed my four rabbits and six hens."

Wheels and Deals

OLE Olsen with Barry
Briggs before the start
of a Wills Internationale
at Wimbledon

5 – Ole and some wheeler-dealing

SPEEDWAY is a sport where it helps to be a wheeler-dealer. It helps a lot. It's a cut-throat game where there are ways and means of getting what you want and who you want.

The biggest deal I ever pulled was in 1976 when I was the Hull promoter and got £15,000 from Coventry for World Champion Ole Olsen. He never cost me a penny to sign and never rode a single race for me.

If you take inflation into account, that must remain as speedway's all-time record transfer because £15,000 then translates into a six or even seven-figure fee now.

But, first, let me explain how the Great Dane, who had won his second World title in 1975, came to be on the Hull books anyway because that is a story on its own.

Team strengths have always been controlled in speedway in an effort to keep them as even as possible and so provide good competition. Today it is achieved through riders being graded according to their averages with a limit on the combined total of those points.

It was different in 1976 where we used the highly contentious Rider Control system. Top men, in particular, would be allocated to clubs in an effort to keep team strengths equal, with the stronger sides forced to surrender a star to a lesser one.

Whatever battles we fought on track during a season, they were nothing like the confrontations that took place down in the basement room of the Speedway Control Board offices in Belgrave Square, London, where we met in the autumn for the annual Rider Control showdown. You hardly dared go to the toilet in case you'd lost a couple of riders and been given a couple of duffers by the time you got back.

The management committee of the British Speedway Promoters' Association were responsible for the divvying up of riders in a system that lasted for quite a few years and always caused many, many heated problems.

In 1975 I'd wanted a particular Swedish rider, Tommy Johansson, and I'd been told in advance of the meeting I couldn't have him. It was any promoter's right to ask for a secret ballot on anything.

I rang Ann Gillespie, who was secretary of the BSPA, and asked her to take a lot of pieces of paper to the Rider Control meeting. She asked me why. I told her I was going to ask for a secret ballot on absolutely every decision that was taken all day.

I didn't tell her that my idea was to wear down the other promoters so I got Johansson but that's what it was. She told me that it would make a hard day even harder but I said that at least I was warning her so she wouldn't run out of voting paper and have to fetch some more.

Reg Fearman was the BSPA chairman and when he asked for the minutes of the previous meeting to be approved I asked for a secret ballot. He asked why and I said I wanted one and that it was my right to have one.

The meeting started at around 10.30 and I asked for a ballot on every single item we discussed all day long. I brought up all kinds of subjects, although rider allocation was the prime topic of the meeting, but eventually I wore them down and got the vote for the rider I wanted. It was past midnight when we left the building. Not the first, or last, time in my career, I wasn't very popular.

That's one of the reasons why, when we have promoters' meetings now, the only items that can be discussed are those on the agenda. You can't throw new subjects on the table and there's no such thing as 'Any Other Business'.

The art of a meeting used to be to get the other promoters fed up and wear them out so you could get something contentious accepted. The trick wasn't just to ask for secret ballots but to get it placed at the bottom of agenda, or bring it up under Any Other Business, so you could get it pushed through when all people wanted to do was to go home. But it can't happen like that nowadays.

That is the background of how Rider Control meetings worked and when we came together the year after the Johansson affair, to arrange team strengths for the 1976 season, it caused bigger after-shocks than ever before with me right in the middle of them.

We had a rider called Jimmy McMillan, a lovely lad who is now the Machine Examiner at Coventry and an International Motor Federation official. He was allocated to Wolverhampton and their star man, Ole Olsen, was given to us.

He was the World Champion so I was more than happy about that but that was only the start of things, not the end.

In fairness I have to say, at this juncture, that Ole disagrees with all my recollections of what happened in the weeks that followed 30 years ago but this is my honest account of the intrigue and aggravation that took place.

I telephoned Ole when he'd become a Hull rider and arranged to go down to his Cheshire home at Holmes Chapel to discuss a contract. We sat for two or three hours and agreed a financial deal in principle.

Ole will deny that we even talked about how he'd like the track to be prepared. But, a few weeks later, my happiness at having a world class rider on my books was shattered when he telephoned and told me he wouldn't come to Hull. I told him he'd been allocated and had to come.

Then the late Charles Ochiltree, who was the promoter at Coventry, started to ring regularly asking me if I would agree to release Ole and I kept telling him that I wouldn't.

I informed the Promoters' Association that Olsen was refusing to come to Hull under the allocation system. They said that if he didn't come I could have a rider replacement or guest facility for him all year. I wasn't going to be hung out to dry and I was quite prepared to sit him out because if he didn't ride for us, he didn't ride for anyone.

I was very much at the bottom of a popularity poll with Ole and Charles. It's fair to say that Ole and myself were never bosom buddies but he was a brilliant speedway rider and that's what I wanted, a speedway rider - not a pal.

I knew that Ole was staying in Pasadena, California, on holiday. I made an appointment with him to fly over with my then business partners, Wally Mawdsley and Brian Larner, in the hope of making one final attempt to sort out the whole mess and persuade him to come to Hull.

I was aware that, out of the speedway season, Ole liked a rum and coke. We met him at his hotel and the plan was that I'd do the talking and Larner would keep the rum and cokes flowing in the hope of it helping him to change his mind.

But he kept saying no, it got heated and I told him he'd spend the 1976 season sitting on the fence because Hull weren't going to give in, especially as we'd already got a facility to replace him. But the trip was a waste of time and money as far as Ole was concerned although we did do another great piece of business while we were over there which I will come to in the next chapter.

We came back home and, eventually, Charles Ochiltree telephoned me to ask if we could have a meeting to discuss the whole situation. I told him I couldn't see much point but agreed to do it and we got together in the Post House hotel, just off the M6 between Stoke and Stafford.

Wheels and Deals

There were four of us there. Ochiltree and Olsen, myself and Larner who I told to let me do the talking. Charles suggested we had a private room and I said that was fine as long as he paid for it. It wasn't all he finished up paying for.

I'd already told him that Ole would have to miss the season if he wouldn't ride for Hull. Charles opened the meeting by asking what kind of fee we'd want.

I said not a penny less than £15,000 and they both nearly fell off their chairs onto the floor. That's a lot of money now, never mind 30 years ago.

When we went into the meeting I was prepared to drop a bit with £12,000 being the absolute bottom line.

But something happened during the meeting that I'll never, ever forget. Ole pointed at me and said: 'Listen, little man.' That annoyed me intensely. I told him that remark had just cost Charles Ochiltree £3,000 because, until then, I was prepared to bend a bit. After that it was £15,000 or no deal and he wouldn't be allowed to ride for anyone else.

Charles said he wouldn't pay that much and I said it was his prerogative. Olsen was fuming. I wasn't too happy. I am little but he didn't mean it in that manner when he pointed at me. Civility costs nothing.

They asked to leave the meeting for a while and went outside. They came back in and Charles said: 'Okay, I'll pay £15,000.'

I asked for it to be put in writing, which upset him. But I said I needed it in writing within 48 hours and then I'd be prepared to contact the BSPA and release Olsen. And that's what happened.

Even now, when I drive on the M6 I look up at that hotel and think: 'That's where I got £15,000 for Ole Olsen and he never rode for me.'

I've signed a lot of riders in my career and most of the deals have been straight forward. One or two, like the Olsen transfer, haven't.

One such example was when I signed Nigel Crabtree as a very young rider from Scunthorpe but the problems in agreeing a deal were based in the fact that their promoter, Brian Osborn, and I didn't get on with each other. And that's an understatement.

I was at Newcastle and we were both Monday night tracks but, because they were the senior side, we had to give way and move to a Sunday when we rode against them with the return at Quibell Park the next night.

Osborn gave me so much aggro on one occasion when they came to Newcastle it was untrue and they only scored about 20 points from

13 races. There were a lot of delays and, because it was a glorious sunny day, the track finished up like a dust bowl.

I hate sending my punters home covered in shale so I was far from happy. I had words with Osborn at the end and told him: 'Don't forget we're coming to you tomorrow – and what goes around comes around.'

One of my riders, a New Zealand lad called Graeme Stapleton who I had a lot of time for, heard it and said: 'He's in for it.'

Graeme was a lad who would do anything for me. Don't ask me where the idea came from but I asked him if he could get six live wild rabbits and bring them to Scunthorpe with him. To my amazement, he said he would.

When I got to Scunthorpe I discovered our meeting was being preceded by the monthly Silver Helmet match race championship. John Jackson was the challenger, I forget who was the holder, and the referee was Bob Owen who King's Lynn promoter Cyril Crane used to call my uncle because he seemed to give a lot of decisions in my favour.

Anyway, I owed Osborn one – or two – for spoiling my meeting the previous day so I took a tape measure out onto the track and measured the height of the safety fence. It had to be a minimum of four feet high to meet the Speedway Control Board regulations.

I found a low spot, called Bob Owen down to look at it and he told Osborn it had to be lifted before racing could start. Bob didn't help matters by telling me to let him know when I was happy with it! Finally, it was acceptable just after the scheduled start time.

The Mayor of Scunthorpe was a guest at the meeting and, when he came out to the track to be presented to the riders, Stapleton let the rabbits loose on the centre green while everyone was watching the official party.

It was chaos. Obviously the meeting couldn't start with wild rabbits running around and they aren't the easiest of things to catch. I reckon it was another 20 minutes before the meeting started and I'm not sure, until now, if anyone knew where those rabbits came from apart from Graeme and myself.

I thought touché. It's something we should all remember in this game because if you stitch someone, you've always got to go back to his track at some time in the future.

Scunthorpe had a novice at that time called Nigel Crabtree and I thought I saw a rider with real potential. I wanted to buy him from Brian as one for the future but, not helped by our personal relationship, we couldn't agree a fee.

Wheels and Deals

He was just coming into the Scunthorpe team but we agreed that I would pay £100 for every point of his average at the end of the season. When it arrived the figure was 0.61 so I signed Nigel for the princely sum of £61 – and sold him a few years later for £6,000.

You sign riders on their potential and some you win, some you lose. This one I won!

More recently, I transferred Jan Jaros from Belle Vue to King's Lynn for – wait for it – two all-day breakfasts! And, before I go any further, that is in no way a reflection on the youngster's ability.

When Tony Mole bought Belle Vue at the end of 2004, and installed me as co-promoter and team manager, we discovered that Jan was on our retained list although he hadn't been in the team at the end of the season.

Even before that, Buster Chapman, the promoter at King's Lynn who is a real hard worker and a man for whom I've a lot of time, had claimed that Jan was his asset. He had taken the matter to the British Speedway Promoters' Association management committee for adjudication and they came down on the side of Belle Vue.

Buster wasn't happy at all. And when Buster's not happy you know about it. He approached Tony and myself. Legally, he was Belle Vue's rider but we agreed that, morally, he belonged to King's Lynn.

We asked Buster what he'd give us for him and we received a two-word answer. But they serve a good all-day breakfast at King's Lynn so we said he could buy us two and he said okay.

Mind you, it was a bad deal for me because, since I moved from Workington to Belle Vue, I haven't needed to go to King's Lynn any longer so I never did collect that breakfast.

But, looking at it as a businessman, it is going up in value all the time!

6 – *Briggo: the most popular Viking*

THE little plot to feed Ole Olsen a few rum and cokes before talking him into signing for Hull was an expensive failure, as I described in the previous chapter.

It was 1976 and I was in Pasadena, California with my co-promoters, Wally Mawdsley and Brian Larner, with nothing to show for our trip apart from airline and hotel bills, not to mention the bar bill!

The prospect of going home red-faced and empty-handed, with no good news for our Hull supporters, was not one we fancied. Something had to be done.

Enter Barry Briggs. The four-times World Champion, Kiwi legend and one of speedway's greatest-ever draw cards was having a quiet holiday with his family and friends at his Californian cliff-top home at Dana Point. It is the most beautiful spot, south of Los Angeles on the way down to San Diego.

His neighbours included Tab Hunter, the actor and singer famous for his 1950s hits Young Love and Red Sails in the Sunset, as well as British athletics golden girl Mary Rand. She won Olympic gold in the long jump in Tokyo in 1964 when she was known as Mary Bignal.

So Briggo was settled in a fabulous place, surrounded by his family and beautiful people. And why shouldn't he have been taking it easy in the Californian sun? After all, he was the retired Barry Briggs. Or, at least, that's what he thought. One thing he most definitely wouldn't have been thinking about was Hull speedway.

Let's be honest, who could think of Hull when you are relaxing in a beautiful home overlooking a picturesque harbour and the Pacific Ocean? Well, I can tell you that Hull speedway was exactly what we were thinking about when we knocked on his door.

Before we had left for America, I had taken the trouble to check out that Briggo was in town and, in fact, Speedway Star Editor Philip Rising was staying with him at the time. They knew we were paying a visit but Briggo certainly didn't know what we might be coming for – but he soon did.

I was aware he was a UK tax exile and, obviously, everyone in speedway knew he had retired from Wimbledon. Even so, I had taken the precaution of asking Cyril Maidment, the Dons' team manager and promoter, for permission to make an approach to Briggo because he was still their rider.

Cyril agreed and we even settled on a loan fee of £750 if we signed him. I asked him to keep it quiet because I had only planned to speak to Briggo if we failed to sign Olsen.

We made an appointment to visit him and were sitting outside enjoying a glass of wine when I suddenly dropped it on his toes: "Will you make a comeback and ride for Hull next season?" Until then he hadn't got a clue that was why we were there.

Junie, his lovely late wife, and their two lads, Tony and Gary, were as gobsmacked as Briggo whose first reaction was to say no. But I started working on him. I've always said bull beats brains and I think it did in this case. I just kept talking and talking about why he should ride for Hull.

Briggo asked us to go back the next day. He probably wanted to talk to Junie about it and I don't think she was too pleased about what we wanted. But we went back and Briggo said he'd give it a go if we could do a deal.

He asked me what we would expect from him if he signed and I told him we'd want a nine-point average, a target which he achieved. We got fairly close to a deal but we weren't quite getting there and I certainly wasn't going to lose him at that point. I always try to have an ace card, or a tiebreaker, up my sleeve in case I need it and I played that by telling him he could have a farewell meeting at the end of the season, the equivalent of a testimonial. That clinched it. The great Barry Briggs was a Hull rider.

He said that he couldn't live in England at that time for tax reasons so he planned to base himself in Germany and do a few meetings there as well. I told him he could fly into Manchester airport on a Wednesday, we'd pick him up and take him to Hull for the meeting and then he could stay with me before flying out again the next morning. We also arranged for Eric Boocock to look after the bikes Briggo would ride. Eric's equipment was always immaculate, not something you could always say about Briggo!

He said we'd sort out paying for the air tickets as we went along but I'd worked out what they would cost and it was horrendous. I told him I'd rather pay him a fee for his season's travel so he said he'd make a phone call for advice. I can only say he was badly advised because the fee he wanted was miles out – air miles out.

If you asked him now about airfares and Ian Thomas he'd talk to you for ages about it! But we'd agreed a fee to be paid in monthly instalments and that it was it.

I can admit now that signing Briggo was partly for business and partly for me. I had started watching speedway at Bradford in 1949 and, during the fifties, I used to go with my dad on the BOB's Club bus. That was the Bradford, Otley and Burley club and I remember Briggo coming up to race.

In those days riders took part in three World Championship qualifiers and he came to Odsal for his last round needing a 15-point maximum to get through because his previous two meetings had been nightmares. He didn't make a decent start all night but he won his five races after knocking riders all over the place. From that day I was a fan. He was hard, a great rider to watch and an entertainer so I was both promoter and fan when I signed him.

When the season started his whole family came over and I'd arranged for the official signing of his contract to be done live on Yorkshire TV. Arthur Scargill, the leader of the Miners' Union, was in the hospitality suite where we went before the programme. He just looked at us and said: "Who are you?" I said: "Nobody, who are you?" I never did like him.

Since then, the Thomas and Briggs families have been friends and my wife, Dot, and Junie were in touch a lot until Briggo lost her so tragically.

Mind you, having him stay with us after meetings caused us a problem or two. Briggo was very partial to avocados and they weren't easy to find in those days. Dot used to tramp round all the local supermarkets trying to find them for him. I don't think she'd do it these days.

More bizarrely, one of our female supporters at Hull just loved Briggo being in the team. So much so that, when she discovered he stayed overnight at our house, she asked Dot if she could buy the sheets off his bed. Dot refused, of course, but I always said she should have sold them and let him sleep on the mattress if it meant making a few quid!

We used to run the Yorkshire TV Trophy during the 1970s before we signed Briggo. It was a big meeting that went out on TV and we always booked some of the top guys like him, Ivan Mauger and Ole Olsen.

I did a deal with Briggo to ride in it and he won his first race but, when he came back into the pits, he flopped down in a heap. We called Dr. Scott, God bless him, to have a look and he immediately pulled him out of the meeting because of a dodgy virus. I don't know what it was but he certainly didn't need to be riding a speedway bike.

Wheels and Deals

I'd paid him up front when he arrived at the track because he'd been on a guarantee. You don't do that with a lot of people but with him you could. He was looking very much the worse for wear but he came to find me when he'd got changed and returned the envelope containing his fee.

I asked him why he was doing that and he said it was because he hadn't done his job. I told him it wasn't his fault and to keep it. After all, he'd turned up and was declared ill. It was no different from going out to race and getting injured. He told me: "That's very fair. The next time you book me I'll do it for half price." And he did. That explains why I rate the bloke so highly because, for me, Briggo was so much more than the great rider who had captured my imagination as a youngster.

We never had a written contract when he rode for Hull, it was all verbal. His word was his bond and we never had any problems with that kind of agreement. We had good working and social relationships but he was never universally popular with promoters because of the fees he wanted to ride in open meetings and the same applied to Ivan Mauger. I could never subscribe to that point of view because it wasn't compulsory to book them. I believe that you should never fall out with anyone when you are negotiating and, if you can't do a deal, you just walk away from it.

I like to supplement my speedway meetings with occasional guest appearances and I booked Freddie Starr to come to Hull for Briggo's first meeting. I think Freddie is a genius. He came into the office and he could tell straight away that my secretary, Lesley, wasn't a fan. He said straight out: "You don't like me do you?" She replied: "No."

So he started doing impressions. I think he's a brilliant, funny man and I was crying with laughter. Lesley didn't raise a smile as he went through six or seven of his impersonations. Then he did the American actor Jack Palance and, thankfully, she cracked up.

Freddie was interested in speedway and had sponsored Reg Wilson at Sheffield. He was appearing at Batley Variety Club so it wasn't a problem for him to come across to Hull for the meeting where the whole Briggs family had also turned up. I was trying to arrange with Freddie what he was going to do and he told me to leave it to him. We hadn't agreed a fee when I booked him and when I asked him how much I owed him he said: "Give me a Briggo anorak." I thought that wasn't a bad deal.

Briggo was the club's big signing and the place was packed for his first meeting. I'd arranged the big entrance with the rest of the team lining up on the centre green before he came out on his own and rode slowly round the track waving to the fans. Great plan, I thought, to get the maximum drama out of the great man's arrival on Humberside. But Freddie had different ideas. The trouble was that I'd told Briggo to ride out slowly and Freddie could run that fast. He ran level with him for the whole lap shouting to the crowd: "He's a puff, he's a puff."

It wasn't the scenario I'd planned but it went down brilliantly with the fans. That was just as well because Freddie hadn't finished with him. I gave Briggo the mike to say a few words but our other Starr pinched it off him and tied him up with the cable. It was chaos.

Freddie was such fun but we saw the other side of him before the night was out and that was so sad. It had been publicised that he'd been having personal problems but he invited us all back to the Batley club after the meeting. The Briggs family were staying with us so we all went to Batley and not only were our names on the door; we were shown to a best table.

We watched his show, went backstage afterwards and then sat and talked until five o'clock in the morning. He had us in stitches when he came up with a way to stop riders breaking the tapes and that was to make them out of barbed wire! But, underneath all that, he seemed a sad and lonely man and, when we said it was time to go, he tried to get us to stay even longer.

The year Briggo was at Hull was the only year that I ever won anything in my era as the promoter there. It was in the Inter League Cup and we were drawn at Berwick. Briggo insisted that it wasn't in his deal that he had to go to ride there. I told him he had to go and we went on arguing about it for some time leading up the meeting.

Berwick, of course, were desperate to have him riding at their track. The promoters were Mrs. Elizabeth Taylor and Kenny Taylor and they said that if I could get him to go, he could stay for the night in a castle up there on the Scottish borders. The owner was a speedway fan and would be delighted to have him there. I threw that into the argument and it was the clincher. He rode in the meeting and slept in a castle!

I'd promised Briggo his farewell meeting at the end of 1976 as part of his deal and, when the night came, the weather was terrible. We'd pulled in a top class field but I was surprised at some of the top riders who didn't want the meeting to go ahead because the conditions weren't good. They included Mauger and Peter Collins, who were his mates. But we did run it, there was a good crowd and he made a few quid out of it.

Wheels and Deals

One of the things that amazed me about Briggo's level of success was the fact that his bikes could look in need of a bit of tender loving care. They were obviously okay because of the level at which he was competing and he always denied there was anything wrong with them.

But, especially compared with Mauger's bikes, they could look worse for wear with bits wired up. He was similar to Ove Fundin because his gear wasn't always the best to look at. I'd never knock Briggo because of what he achieved. There are only three people who have won more World titles than him but it does make you wonder if Barry could have won more if his machinery had been as immaculate as Mauger's. Who knows?

He was World class and I remember top speedway journalist Peter Oakes writing an article saying that if you went out on the streets to conduct a survey to find speedway's most famous rider, Briggo would come out top. He felt that part of the reason was his BB initials but whatever the reasons he was a sporting superstar. If he played soccer now he would be a galactico.

I've had a few spats with Briggo over the years. Like any World Champion, or top class rider, he had his moments. He could be temperamental but so could I and I always found best way to deal with anyone who was like that was to be temperamental back.

Signing Briggo for Hull was a brilliant move and I can honestly say that, in all the years I was at Hull, he was the most popular rider that ever appeared for us. It was a good deal for him, apart from the airfares, and a good deal for us because he pulled in the paying customers.

We have a social relationship, which remains to this day, and I am proud to count him as a friend. One of the places where that friendship developed was on the golf course and Briggo has difficulty in lining up his shots because he lost a finger in a crash during the 1972 World Final at Wembley. He recalls that night for obvious reasons because he missed his chance of his fifth World title, lost a finger and was paid the princely sum of £15 for his efforts!

The missing finger means that it takes him a long time to line up a shot on the golf course. I would get a bit impatient and try to hurry him along but he would have the last word by suggesting that I tried playing with three fingers and a thumb.

I took him to play at my club, Hawksworth at Guiseley, near where I live, and we were on the par three, 174-yard third hole. I hit a good ball and I knew it had gone on the green but it was one of those holes where you couldn't always see where your ball had finished. I said to him, jokingly, that it was a hole in one to which he said a rude word and promised me a big bottle of whisky if it was. When we got to the green there was no ball to be seen. Briggo looked in the hole and said: "I owe you a bottle of scotch."

It was the second hole in one of my golfing career. It took him about six months but he did come up with the whisky. My other hole in one was when I was playing with my son, Lyndon, on another par three at the course. He was really sick about it because he'd never had one and, while he never bought me a bottle, he never told anyone in the clubhouse so I didn't have to buy a round of drinks.

There's one story that sums up Briggo. He has had a colourful life, which includes mining for gold and diamonds. He's always got something on the go and his schemes don't always work out. One example was when Wembley Stadium closed. Everything was auctioned off. Ivan Mauger bought a chandelier while Briggo bought a toilet that was cracked when he took delivery of it.

We're still in touch and I was delighted to be invited to his 70th birthday bash at the golf club near Solihull, which is owned by former Coventry rider, John Harrhy. It was like a Who's Who of speedway.

My abiding memory of him is that he raced his heart out for Hull and for me. I am pleased and proud to be able to say that he rode for me before he retired.

YOUNG Lyndon Thomas with the World Championship trophy, en route to the 1980 World Final in Gothenburg.

'ON LOAN' FROM IVAN MAUGER FOR 12 MONTHS!

ENGLAND'S victorious World Team Cup squad in 1980:
Back row left to right: Ian Thomas (manager), Michael Lee, Chris Morton
and Eric Boocock (Co-manager).
Front: John Davis, Peter Collins and Dave Jessup.

UNTIL next week ... Ian Thomas drops Barry Briggs off at Manchester Airport during Briggos' one season spell at Hull in 1976.

ABOVE: Workington favourite Lou Sansom with comedian Charlie Williams.
BELOW: Ian Thomas and son Lyndon with the World Championship trophy amongst the British press contingent en route home from the 1979 World Final in Katowice, Poland, won by Hull rider Ivan Mauger.

ABOVE: One of the more unusual and tasteful 'acts' booked by Ian Thomas ...
Mister Methane propels a dart from his nether regions to explode the balloon on
the head of Workington boss Tony Mole.
TOP RIGHT: 'Del Boy' and his Reliant Robin on opening night at Derwent Park.
BOTTOM RIGHT: Speedway advertising in the Middle East.

IAN Thomas with Bill Maynard

IAN Thomas with Colin Crompton

IAN Thomas, then England team manager, sprays his boys with champagne
after their World Team Cup win in Poland.

7 – *Ivan: a speedway legend*

IVAN Mauger is a living speedway legend. That probably explains why I bought him from Exeter for £12,000 in 1979 because it was an awful lot of money at the time.

Richard Bott, the top sports journalist who was my Publicity Officer, organised a Press conference at the Piccadilly Hotel in Manchester to announce that we had signed him. I don't know to this day why it was organised in Manchester when he was joining Hull, but we had a tremendous turn-out.

It took three or four days of talks at his home in Bramhall, near Manchester Airport, to conclude the whole package and Ivan will confirm we spent only three or four hours talking about the financial side. That doesn't mean he wasn't expensive because he was. Very expensive.

The rest of the time was spent talking about things he wanted changing at Hull if he was coming to ride for us. I could meet him on some of his requests, like which riders he would like in the team, but there were other things such as changes to the pit area which just weren't practical.

He was such a professional that he'd got everything worked out and, would you believe, that even included his beauty sleep.

Ivan was a great believer in getting his proper rest, despite his hectic schedule, and he had calculated how many more hours he would be able to spend in bed before the World Final the following September if he rode for Hull instead of Exeter. I told him he could go to bed in an afternoon if he was tired and he told me he was talking about real sleep time at night.

That might sound strange, especially coming from a top speedway rider who was always travelling, but he was completely serious. Proper sleep was part of the planning of a man who was totally professional and meticulous in his preparations. Many riders have tried to follow his example with varying degrees of success, but I doubt if many of them counted their hours of sleep.

I have been told that when he was at Belle Vue he'd ignore the pleasures of the Zoo and fairground after a meeting and go home to Bramhall, just down the road. He'd be tucked up in bed while other riders were still at the Hyde Road track having a drink.

Ivan, like Barry Briggs, never had a written contract when he rode

Wheels and Deals

for me at Hull. We had several fall-outs when we were negotiating but they were never to do with the financial aspects of the deal and they were all resolved. It is my experience that riders of their standing can be difficult to deal with on a financial basis but you usually find that, once the terms are agreed, there are no on-going problems. They don't come back asking for extra and wouldn't get it if they did. A deal's a deal.

Ivan and I disagreed over a few things and then sorted them out but I wasn't the only person at Hull to have a fall-out with him because my secretary, Lesley, never got on with him from the day he arrived to the day he left. Lesley, who remains a very good family friend, would make the odd deliberate mistake on his pay sheets just to wind him up.

He used to come up to me on a Wednesday afternoon before a meeting and say: "She's done it again." I would tell him to go in to the office and sort it out but she would keep her head down until he said: "Excuse me, but I think you have made a mistake." I never got to the bottom of the problem but she didn't like him and there was no love lost between them.

I think people could find him arrogant at times and he certainly liked things – such as pay sheets – to be right. There was one British League Riders' Championship at Belle Vue when he wasn't happy with the seats that had been allocated to the wives and girlfriends of the lads who were taking part. Ivan grabbed the centre green microphone on the parade to voice his displeasure about the awful seats and even gave out the phone number of Reg Fearman, the Promoters' Association Chairman, with the invitation to fans to call him. And did they ever. Fearman's phone never stopped ringing for ages and he went nuts about it.

But that was Ivan. He did things the right way and, in return, he expected things affecting him to be done right. That example was something extra he brought to Hull, apart from his points-scoring brilliance on a bike, and many of the boys in the side took the golden chance to learn from the great man at close quarters.

Reg Fearman wasn't the only promoter to be unhappy with him. Like Barry Briggs, and it was probably no coincidence, he wasn't popular due to the fact that he was expensive when anyone wanted to book him for an open meeting. But, as I've said, they didn't have to book him.

He was very expensive for me but no one forced me to sign him. He was a draw card and the away fans loved to boo him. Not that he was bothered about that. He would just say that he wasn't paid to be popular.

No one could knock him for being the ultimate professional and for a young guy to be in the same team as him was an experience they could never buy. There was so much they could learn from watching him prepare in the dressing room and from how he worked in the pits during a match. If they didn't benefit from it, then more fool them.

I know that applies to being in a team with any World class rider but, for me, he's the greatest rider the sport has ever known and I say that in the knowledge that Tony Rickardsson has equalled his record of six World Championships. Joe Owen, who so tragically had a bad crash later on, was one of the riders who really took on board everything he could from having Ivan around.

Mind you, I do know one young rider who failed to benefit from riding alongside Ivan. Me. When I was stumbling around the northern circuit getting second half rides wherever I could I was at Newcastle one night and happened to be in the right place at the right time. Or was I?

I wasn't very good at all and the only odd times I won a race was when other riders broke down. I was at Newcastle for a second half booking but the opposition walked out because they felt it was too wet to ride. Mike Parker, the promoter, had got fans in the stadium and he was determined to put on a show so he got two teams together out of the riders who were left and I was paired with Ivan. I was so proud. I didn't know him personally. What I did know was that he was a speedway idol and I wasn't.

The first time we went out together he said that he was taking gate one. I said I didn't care if I was on the dog track as long as I was in the race with him. I fell off three times at the start of one race and each time the referee put us all back in. Ivan asked me if there was any chance of me doing all four laps and I said: "I'll do my best Mr. Mauger." I got paid for my efforts but I would have ridden for nothing that night.

It's funny that all those years later I should finish up as his promoter. He could get on a line at times but who doesn't in a high-pressure sport like speedway? I've seen him mad many times but I've never seen him as furious as he was the night we went to Coventry needing a draw to win the 1979 British League championship.

We'd lost Kelly Moran to a broken collarbone and had brought in Graeme Stapleton. We were part of a double header as Coventry were riding against Leicester the same night so the stadium was packed.

Wheels and Deals

The only thing that mattered to us was not to lose but we went down by a few points and waved goodbye to the title.

However, we all knew that the meeting hadn't been lost at Coventry stadium. It had been lost at previous away meetings when Frank Auffrett, Graham Drury and Bobby Beaton had not turned up and we'd lost.

Ivan was absolutely livid afterwards in that Coventry dressing room, ironically the same one where the balloon had gone up when Kenny Carter said he wanted a British Final to go ahead, despite the conditions. Believe me, there were steel shoes, helmets and boots flying about. He wasn't annoyed at losing to Coventry, although we probably would have won with Kelly in the side; it was the fact that riders hadn't turned up for other matches when they should.

That would have made Ivan angry in any circumstances but fuel was added to the ire by the fact it made Hull the only British track where he never won the League championship. It spoiled his record and he couldn't forgive it. He still mentions it when we meet.

That wasn't the only time I've seen him in a temper but it was the worst. He came off the pit phone one night at Hull after talking to the referee and was he not happy. He threw the phone – my phone! – onto the ground and smashed it. I told him that the cost of replacing it would come off his pay sheet and he fired back that he'd ask for a transfer if it did. I said: "Please yourself, but it is coming off." It was deducted but he never did ask for a transfer.

I've never made any secret of the fact that I've pulled a few strokes in my time and I'm afraid I'll have to keep some of them to myself. I also like a bet and one that gave me a real buzz was when I went to the 1979 World final in Katowice, Poland, when Hull had Ivan and Kelly Moran in the field. The champion won a £500 first prize in those days and I set myself the challenge of making more money than Ivan on the day. If he won his sixth title, which he did, I wanted to be able to go up to him and say: "Congratulations – and would you believe I made more out of you winning the championship than you did?"

He was on offer at 6-1 with the bookies so I put £100 on him to do it, which was a damned big bet in those days. I told him on the way from the hotel to the post-match reception that I'd made £600 out of his victory and he didn't like it at all. No, not at all!

It was a great end to a day that had started with the ultimate contrast of the most chilling, dreadful experience of my life. Lada Cars were the Hull sponsors and their top man in Britain, David Usher and his

Wheels and Deals

No 2, Ken Robinson, came to the final along with my secretary, Lesley. In the morning of the meeting we decided to go to see the notorious Auschwitz concentration camp.

We all came out crying. It was unbelievable. Everybody in the world should have to go there once to witness the atrocities. We were so depressed and yet less than 12 hours later there was the euphoria of having Ivan and Kelly finishing first and fourth in the world. I've never known such a contrast of emotions in one day.

I'd read about Auschwitz but nothing can prepare you for going there. I saw somebody digging a heel into the grass so I did. It was white underneath. The guy came and told me it was human bones. The Pope had just been and the flowers that had been laid by relatives of people who died there were still fresh. There was a carpet of human hair, huge piles of spectacles and the gas chambers where people died in their thousands.

I knew about the most amazing thing of a visit there because I'd read about it. But it was still absolutely remarkable. That was the fact that no birds fly in there. They are singing and flying 20 or 30 yards outside but they won't go in. How do they know? Incredible. I never want to go there again but I'm glad I went.

Barry Briggs never touched an alcoholic drink as a rider and still doesn't. Ivan liked people to think he was tee-total but, on occasions, he would let his hair down such as the party we had back at the hotel with his entourage and the Press lads, who were staying at the same hotel, after his 1979 World title win.

He did have the odd drink at the odd time such as the end-of-season Hull dinner dance. Ivan and his wife Raye were going to stay at our house afterwards so he picked up Dot and myself in his Mercedes on the way through from Manchester. It was a cracking do and there was no question of Ivan or myself driving. We'd had a few and the two ladies hadn't.

Ivan and I got in the back of the car, happy but not legless. Raye was driving and Ivan told her it would need some petrol so she stopped and the two girls got out. It was the time when petrol stations were becoming self service and they managed to fill it up but it was a different story when it came to paying.

They'd got a £10 note but what to do with it was a different story. They even tried to push it up the nozzle of the petrol pump before they worked it out. Ivan and I were in stitches watching them but it's fair to say that they didn't see the joke. I still smile every time I pass that garage.

Barry Briggs and Ivan used to ride in Germany at weekends before all the foreign leagues like Poland and Sweden became so strong. It used to annoy me intensely that we could get a wet night in the United Kingdom and they would want the meeting called off but they would ride through three feet of mud in Germany. They could never tell me why but I can only assume that it was for a couple of grand.

It was a privilege and a pleasure to be able to watch Ivan ride, home and away, for a whole season. A lot of people said he was boring to watch due to the fact that he didn't miss many starts and won many races from the gates. But I wouldn't agree with that. He was a craftsman on a bike and I just enjoyed watching him go round four laps of a track.

But my immense admiration of Ivan wasn't solely based on the fact that he was a magnificent professional and a multi-World Champion. It goes back to when he first came across from New Zealand with Raye, a pocketful of dreams and very little else. When he rode for Mike Parker at Newcastle they were living in a flat in Moss Side, Manchester and, to be polite, it was the pits. But he was self-centred, so determined, stubborn and nothing was going to stand in his way of being the world's best. And nothing did.

A word of praise was worth a million if it came from Ivan. He was at Belle Vue as a special guest with the Aces' other previous World Champions, Ove Fundin and Peter Collins, when Tony Mole and I held our opening night at Kirkmanshulme Lane last year.

He said a few words to the crowd and then walked across to me, shook my hand and said: "Well done, Ian." I can't say how much that meant coming from him. It was a big, big compliment and I appreciated it because he didn't throw them out very often.

I see him at functions and I've noticed that if he is wearing a bow tie, it is designed with the little black and white squares that were the trademark on his bikes, helmets and leathers when he was riding. Like I said, he paid great attention to detail and still does.

One of Ivan's team-mates at Hull was Frank Auffrett, a smashing lad from Middlesbrough, who could be relied on to give 100 per cent. I had a lot of time for Frank, a soft spot you might say.

And that makes my next little tale all the more remarkable. I took a run out to Skipton, in the Yorkshire Dales, with Dot last September – it was the day England played in Wales in the World Cup. We were walking round a shop and I had just bought a Speedway Star magazine. For no apparent reason I started thinking about Frank. I hadn't seen him or spoken to him for years but I recalled he had suffered something of a nervous breakdown after giving up speedway.

I walked out of the shop, down Skipton High Street, and a bloke came up to me and said: "Hello." I have to admit it happens to me quite a lot. I stared at him. "You don't know who I am, do you?" he asked. I had to shake my head. I hadn't a clue.

He said: "I'm Frank Auffrett." Strewth.

He owned a boat and was cruising on the Leeds-Liverpool Canal. We went back there, sat in the sun for a couple of hours with a cup of tea and talked about speedway. That brings me back to Ivan.

Frank, and some of the other boys, were in awe of him, even though he was a teammate. Ivan used to take them to meetings abroad on occasions and they were so shy they would draw straws NOT to sit by him on the plane. Frank reckons he usually lost.

When Ivan was celebrating his 40th birthday, fans and riders at Hull bought him gifts to mark the occasion. Frank wanted to buy him something. But what do you get for a man with a gold bike, gold watch and a gold cutlery canteen? It was Hull Fair that week, a huge gathering that I hated because my gate went down. Frank went along to the Fair and came back with – a goldfish.

He gave it to Ivan and it cracked him up. I don't suppose anyone had ever given him a goldfish before. He even thought of building a pond for it in his garden but, finally, he gave it to the kids next door.

It tickled me when I thought about Frank when I got home. He'd spent his younger days tearing round speedway tracks the length and breadth of Britain and here he was, doing about two miles an hour on a canal longboat.

IAN Thomas with Telford co-promoter and former Hull rider Graham Drury

The Moran brothers, Shawn left and Kelly right

8 – *The Yanks Are Coming*

I FEEL the sport of speedway as a whole owes me a debt of gratitude for fetching the marvellous madcap Moran brothers out of the remote world of Californian racing and letting them loose on the World stage.

Yes, people can claim that they were so talented that Kelly and Shawn would have made it over the Pond anyway. That's true enough.

Other people may claim that I'd have done better to leave the pair of hell-raisers where they were but that's rubbish.

The facts of the matter are that I got my backside over to America on several occasions, while others sat and watched. I scouted the scene intensely and brought over a supply of Americans to British speedway who subsequently benefited a number of other tracks. On occasions, those tracks were run by promoters who were happy enough to let me spend my money discovering the riders and were equally happy to cash in on them once they had proved they could do the business over here. Are you listening John Berry? I'll come back to that in the next chapter.

I'll talk about the Moran boys here and then look at the other Yanks I brought over to these shores, notably the brilliant Dennis Sigalos whose talents were noted by the aforementioned Mr. Berry.

There was only one Kelly Moran and I don't know whether or not it's a good thing, but there will never be another. He seemed to spend his life getting into and out of scrapes but I could forgive him anything when I saw him on a bike. He was a genius. I agree with people, up to a point, who say it's a shame that he didn't win more because his talent deserved it. But Kelly was happy doing things his way and nothing would ever change him. I soon realised there was no point in trying to change him.

I brought him over to Hull in 1978 and his impact was immediate and electrifying. He ran a seven-point average in that first year and topped eight points a match the next season when he finished fourth in the World Final in Katowice, Poland, before moving on to Birmingham.

When he first came I'd arranged a car for him and I asked to see his driving licence for insurance purposes. I asked him again. And again. He always had an excuse for not having it with him. Then I asked him where he'd passed his test and he said Costa Mesa in Los Angeles.

I found the relevant phone number in Costa Mesa and then made a lot of calls to try to find out when he'd passed it. I had problems because of the confidentiality situation but, in the long run, I established that one of America's top speedway racers didn't have a driving licence.

I thought that with the way he drove, he wasn't going to pass a test in England so I had to take him off the road before we all finished up in trouble. Then I had a rider who could race but couldn't drive and, for the rest of the season, I had to provide him with a driver, which probably made him speedway's only chauffeur-driven star.

Kelly stayed with my secretary, Lesley, for a while. Then we provided him with a flat in Hull. It had a retractable bed that went up into the wall when it wasn't being used. He'd been partying one night in a local pub and I got a message that he wasn't in too good a state. I went along, collected him and took him back to the flat.

He started jumping off the sideboard onto the bed. It suddenly retracted into its wall space, jamming Kelly in the recess where the bed wanted to go. I couldn't pull it down and Kelly was up there, spread-eagled and squealing away for me to get him out. But it just wouldn't move and, in the long run, I had to call out the fire brigade to release him.

Kelly wasn't good with money, he just didn't bother about such things as long as he had some. He usually did because he was making a decent living out of his speedway. But he was the archetypal party animal and he liked to go out for a good time. He once came up to me after a Hull meeting with a cheque for around £400, which was a lot of money in the seventies.

He asked me if I'd cash it for him, which I did. It was probably about 9.45 and we all went into the bar for a drink. About an hour later he was back in the bar asking me if he could borrow some money. The £400 had gone. Where had it gone? I can only guess.

Kelly once had a very bad accident when Hull were racing at Hackney one Friday night. He was in a hell of a state. I went to the local hospital to see him and there are more friendly places in the world than Hackney hospital on a Friday night. I was waiting to be told I could see him and I remember a bloke coming in with a bottle sticking out of the top of his head.

Eventually, I was allowed to see him but he needed a lot of surgical work to have a thigh pinned and he was facing a long stay. Hull were riding at Wimbledon about a fortnight later so, obviously, I went to see him. He was quite perky. He'd got a big bottle of orange juice on his bedside table and, knowing Kelly, I was suspicious so I had a sip. It tasted more like gin to me! Somebody had smuggled it in for him. I took it away with me but I knew full well he'd get another.

The 1979 World Final was a massive event for Hull because Ivan Mauger, who won it, was our rider at the time and so was Kelly, who finished fourth. It really was something to celebrate because too often we were referred to as the team from a back street town and here we were looking down on everyone else with the World Champion and the No. 4 in our team.

Kelly partied at his hotel in Katowice that night and, fair enough, he had more than a few. The trouble came when he realised that the hotel had smart, white plastic seats in the public rooms and he autographed the lot. He might have got away with it in the bar at Hull but not in a Polish hotel. I guess he did in a way because I had to reimburse the Poles for the damage. He even turned up next morning at a military airfield for our charter flight home in a pair of shorts and with a bottle in his hand. The personnel who escorted us onto the plane couldn't believe their eyes but he was entitled to let his hair down because he had turned in an immense performance the day before.

The following Wednesday it was party night at Hull. I wasn't going to let our moment of glory go by without making the most of it. I hired two open-topped Rolls Royces to come round the track with Ivan first and then Kelly. I also bought two 72-piece sets of gold cutlery, which were worth about £700, and they were presented to the two riders as a permanent memento of a proud night for Hull speedway as well as themselves.

The whole celebration went down very well and Ivan, and his wife Raye, were made up with the cutlery presentation. I know that they have still got it at their home on the Australian Gold Coast. But, unfortunately, I couldn't say the same for Kelly. I was coming out of the bar about an hour after the meeting and I saw a lady carrying a set of cutlery. It was the same as the ones we'd presented to the riders and I knew it wouldn't be Ivan's.

I said: 'Excuse me, madam, would you mind telling me where you got that cutlery?' She said: 'I bought it off Kelly Moran for £30.' I shook my head and explained to her the significance of the gift we had made to Kelly. I asked her to do me a favour and sell it back to me for £50. She understood where I was coming from and, in fact, she only took the £30 she'd paid.

There was no point in giving it back to Kelly so I had it parcelled up and posted it to his father, Tom, in California. I don't know where it is now but I felt it was a very special occasion for Hull and Kelly obviously didn't look at it from the same point of view as Ivan, Raye and myself.

Don't get me wrong, I'm not saying what I did was right and what Kelly did was wrong. It's simply that what was right in my book, and appreciated by the Maugers, had no special significance or place in Kelly's lifestyle and way of doing things. That's the way he was and we've got to respect the fact that he lives his life by his rules, not mine.

I guess everyone has stories to tell about Kelly's antics but, after all that, the reason he was in England was to ride speedway. That's what I paid him to do and, at the end of the day, that is what I am entitled to judge him on and not how he viewed a set of cutlery.

I can sum him up very briefly from that viewpoint because, in my opinion, he was the world's most exciting speedway rider. His balance was incredible but, along with Michael Lee, he was one of the biggest waste of talents that I've ever witnessed in the sport. There was one race in that Katowice World Final when he had got to the stage where he wouldn't win the title but he could still get onto the rostrum.

I was in the pits basically to look after Ivan, although I was trying to help them both, and Ivan asked me before this particular heat to tell Kelly that he'd got to stop Poland's Zenon Plech, who was his biggest threat for the title. That was one of the best races I've ever seen in my life. There wasn't much more than a yard between them for the whole race with Kelly in front while Plech, who knew all the Polish tracks like the back of his hand, pushed him all the way. They were touching at times but Kelly held him off.

That race didn't give Ivan the title but it certainly helped him as well as Kelly's bid to get on the rostrum. But if ever one race showed me what a genius Kelly was on a bike, it was that one.

When he wasn't suffering the after-effects of his endless partying, you couldn't wish to meet a nicer person than Kelly. I know I'm not the only person to say that and it's such a shame he's remembered for that side of his life as much as his magical skills on a bike.

There was a very sad incident when I brought Bruce Penhall over for the Telford ice meeting in 2003. We arranged an Evening with Penhall the night before which was a question and answer show hosted by journalist Richard Bott. Kelly was also in the country because he'd stayed over after riding in the indoor meeting at Brighton and Bruce was very worried that, knowing he was there, Kelly might come in and spoil the night.

I told him I'd keep an eye on the situation and keep Kelly out if he arrived the worse for wear. He did turn up and, unfortunately, he did justify Bruce's fears. I had to leave him outside and while it was the right thing to do for the benefit of the people who had come to listen to Bruce, it made me very, very sad indeed.

I hadn't the heart to keep him out for the autograph session which followed so he came in afterwards but it was such a contrast with Bruce who had still got that wonderful charisma he displayed in his racing days. But I still have no regrets whatsoever for letting Kelly loose on the British or World scene.

I first brought brother Shawn across in October 1979, just before the end of the season, and I was in trouble almost as soon as he'd sat on a bike for me. The idea was I'd have a look at him in action around the Hull circuit and he could take a look at us and at England before anyone made commitments.

He had what was the ultimate recommendation for me because I'd spoken to my American spy George Wenn, who said he was outstanding for his age, and also had a chat with his father, Tom, a lovely man.

Tom was happy for Shawn to follow Kelly to England and my first commitment as far as he was concerned was to send a cheque to the Speedway Control Board after being fined for riding him under an assumed name. I had a four-team tournament between Hull, Sheffield, Exeter and an American Select side but Shawn didn't have the right paperwork and permits so I put him in the programme as David East and also raced him in the second halves of some league matches under that name.

I was sure no-one would find out but Shawn rode Kelly's bike in the four-team event, scored six points and someone guessed who David East really was. I guess I was pushing my luck and, although I never found out exactly how I was rumbled, I was and had to pay a fine of £100. I don't know why I picked on the name East, perhaps it was because my money went West!

Shawn was fined as well by his American Association but it was a small price to pay because he was an immense talent and he came back the following season to start his outstanding British career. That price was made even smaller because of the priceless publicity we received with the story even making National newspaper headlines.

I had first realised his potential when I saw him, at the age of 17, finish second to Bruce Penhall in the American Longtrack championship at Ascot in California. He was flying. That was early in 1979 and I'd flown out to see Kelly, who was recovering from injury, and to take a look at younger brother Shawn while I was there.

Wheels and Deals

I was impressed with his incredible potential. Like Kelly, he was a natural on a bike but I felt he needed another season to improve his learning curve on the American tracks before tackling the British scene. We struck a gentleman's verbal agreement that he would stay home for 1979 and join us the next season which he did – apart from the crazy David East interlude! Shawn only spent the 1980 season at Hull before moving on to ride for Sheffield for nine seasons. He wasn't as wild as Kelly off the track. I always found him a nice kid and I didn't have too many problems with him although, sadly, they did catch up with him later in his career.

He was extremely popular with the crowd, always smiling and I was so sorry he hadn't made more money out of his British career when he finally called it a day and went home for keeps.

I felt a personal element of sadness about the careers of both the Morans. I'm sure they will see my comments from another angle because of their different lifestyles, but I do wish they'd had more to show for their careers over here in real terms when they called it a day and went home to California.

Shawn had finished second to Sweden's Per Jonsson in the 1990 World Final at Bradford. But he was stripped of that honour after providing a positive drugs sample at the Overseas Final earlier in the year. He was such a talented rider and, for his faults, a very pleasant fellow. But when he was preparing to go home for good a year later he didn't have much money and Graham Drury and myself bought all the trophies off him that he'd won in Britain and on the Continent. I can't remember how much we gave him for them but at least he had some money in his pocket when he arrived home.

I'd much preferred he'd been able to go home with his silverware and a healthy bank balance.

9 – The Yanks: second coming

FEW people forget their wedding day and I'm no exception. But I'll never forget the day that American rider Eddie Ingels tied the knot, either.

It attracted national TV and newspaper coverage and it was all down to one of my bright ideas, one that I was starting to wish I'd never had before everything came up trumps on the day.

Speedway promoters have to do all sorts of jobs to keep their tracks in the public eye. But how many have gone out knocking doors looking for a vicar to conduct a ceremony at a speedway track? Or built an altar on the centre green? Well I have.

Ingels was different from the Americans I brought into British speedway because he came to ride for me at Newcastle in 1984 while the rest of the Yanks rode at Hull. Ingels arrived the year I took the Diamonds up into the British League and he was a virtual ever present in a side which included Joe Owen, Rod Hunter and David Bargh. He had an average of nearly six points a match, which was a great effort in his first season in the league, and I transferred him to the late Stuart Bamforth at Belle Vue the following season.

Eddie was a lovely lad, who came across with his fiancee, and he wanted to get married while he was over here. I'm always looking for angles for publicity and this one was far too good to ignore. I asked them if they would like to have the ceremony on the centre green at the Newcastle stadium and, when they showed an interest, I made some enquiries to find someone willing to conduct it

A lot of people turned it down flat but I found a Church of England vicar who said he would come to Brough Park and give the marriage a blessing if they had gone through a legal Register Office wedding first. The official side of it was all arranged and then I decided that if we were going to do, we would do it right.

I told the rest of the team to be there in top hats and tails. The late Kenny Carter, who was riding for Halifax at that time, was best man and we hired a Rolls Royce for the bride. We arranged for an altar to be built on the centre green, invited Newcastle fans to attend, set it up for Kenny to bring Eddie round the track from the pits and I organised an evening reception at a nice place so we could end the day in style.

Our stadium landlords, Ladbrokes, agreed not to charge us rent for the use of the stadium and everything was all ready to go – or so we thought! With 48 hours to go, the vicar telephoned to say his bishop had found out about it and told him he couldn't officiate. Wonderful. I'd sent out all the publicity, Breakfast Time TV were coming down as well as the Tyne Tees and BBC TV stations and all the local media. And no vicar!

I went round a lot of churches and a lot of vicarages, of varying denominations, on the two days before the wedding to try to find a replacement. I finally came up with a man from the Pentecostal Church who said he'd do it if there was an altar and if he could preach a sermon. I was so relieved I told him he could preach for as long as he liked as long as he did the job.

We agreed a fee with him and we were up and running. And, after all that, it went like clockwork. We couldn't have wished for better weather and more than 700 people came along to witness the happy event. We had a collection, because they have them in church, and the money went to the new Mr. and Mrs. Ingels.

Their parents came over. My mum, God bless her, bought a new hat and came along, the minister gave his sermon and everyone went away happy. Yes, I have to admit it started out as a gimmick, which attracted a great deal of publicity, but it was done very tastefully and we didn't do anything to harm the sanctity of marriage.

Eddie was never a star as a rider, more of a steady middle-of-the-road man at Newcastle. He was the same when he went to Belle Vue after the operation at Brough Park had closed down but more about that black hole in my life elsewhere. I don't know where he is now, or what happened to him after he stopped riding in England, but I'd love to meet him again one day.

One thing is certain; neither of us will ever forget his wedding day!

Prior to Newcastle, I had run speedway at Hull for eleven seasons from 1971, the last eight in the top division after I had bought a licence from Coatbridge. I had moved into senior racing in 1974 and for six of those eight seasons I had at least one American in the side. By and large, I loved having the Yanks over here.

Most of them were colourful, a bit loud, charismatic and damned good riders to boot. They certainly brightened up many a forgettable night at The Boulevard. People might ask if signing them was a good excuse for a holiday in California when I went over to find them. I wouldn't argue with that altogether because I loved going there and did so regularly.

The more serious question I was asked as these unknown talents kept arriving on Humberside was how did I keep finding them, and the answer was one that I kept strictly to myself. If other promoters wanted to move in on the American market they could sort it out for themselves and, of course, that's what happened at Cradley Heath when they signed the likes of Bruce Penhall, Bobby Schwartz and Lance King in the late seventies and early eighties.

But I like to think that I was the instigator of bringing over the Americans on a regular basis and I look back at those signings nowadays with mixed feelings.

My big contacts, or talent scouts, in California, were a man called George Wenn and his wife, Freda. George, who died a few years ago, was the man who was involved in making Ivan Mauger's legendary gold-plated bike. My wife, Dorothy, and I became very friendly with them and we used to visit them frequently, tying in a holiday with business.

George was an official at the tracks run by the American promoter, Harry Oxley, and he took us to see the racing at San Bernardino and Costa Mesa where I could get a first-hand look at all these Californian kids. It was like a conveyor belt in those days and while many of the riders out there would never be anything more than enthusiastic amateurs, every now and then that conveyor system would produce a real diamond.

Having said that, my first import in 1974 was by no means my greatest success. It was Steve Gresham and he only did six meetings for me before moving on to find success elsewhere. Unusually for an American, Steve was the exception to the rule amongst the ones I brought across because he didn't have that flamboyance and charisma enjoyed by so many of his fellow countrymen.

I found him to be rather arrogant. I didn't like him too much and he certainly wasn't as good a rider as the Americans who followed him to Hull. But, perhaps, he didn't think too much of me, either, because I have an especially painful memory of meeting up with him again in 1982 when Stuart Bamforth had asked me to take over as team manager at Belle Vue after Eric Boocock had resigned.

Steve was riding for Reading by then and he came up against us soon after I had moved in. He had been involved in a clash with one of my riders during a race and I went out to the pit gate area to remonstrate with him, if remonstrate was the right word, as he came off the track. But he didn't wait for me to say anything because he made the first move and kicked me in my testicles.

Needless to say it hurt and that was why I did a silly thing and retaliated. I guess I should not have struck back at all, being a team manager, but it's hard to ignore a boot in such a tender area and, stupidly, I hit him. Unfortunately for me, Steve was still wearing his crash helmet and a full face mask so, to add insult to injury, I finished up by hurting my hand as well.

Even then, that wasn't the end of the incident because I almost finished up on a charge from the Speedway Control Board, now the Speedway Control Bureau, who are in charge of discipline. As if I hadn't taken enough punishment already! Dick Bracher, the Control Board secretary, put me on a charge for bringing the sport into disrepute when I was more concerned about something more personal being in disrepute.

I wrote back and asked him if he'd ever been kicked that way. I told him it was extremely painful and wasn't merited. I accepted that I had retaliated but said I felt that I had a fair reason for doing it. I added that, if charges were being made, they should have gone to both of us and he dropped the whole matter.

Belle Vue fans still remember that incident because it came up when Tony Mole and I went to a meeting with them at Kirkmanshulme Lane after we had taken over at Belle Vue at the end of 2004.

Steve was a mid-order rider who didn't stay long and the next American to arrive was Mike Curoso two years later. We provided all our Americans with accommodation and we found him a lovely flat in Hull. We thought we'd done him proud but he complained that it only had a shower and no bath and he wanted a move. Brian Larner, my partner at the time, went nuts at him and said that if he thought he was going to have time to lie in the bath all day, then he'd better think again. He stayed there.

Curoso was involved in a fight with team-mate Graham Drury, who is now my partner in the annual ice speedway meetings at Telford, in front of the whole crowd at a home meeting. They were arguing about gate positions because, in those days, they weren't set like they are now. The team manager and senior rider usually settled who went off which gate but both Graham and Mike wanted the same starting position.

I certainly wasn't happy about them having a punch-up in front of the fans and I was even less happy when it hit the Press in a big way. I called the pair of them into the office and told them I didn't mind if they wanted to have a fight but, if there was ever a next time, to do it behind the stand when there was no-one else around. I kept Curoso for a couple of seasons. Like Gresham, he was middle order rider and, finally, I sold him on to Poole.

Kelly Moran was the next American to wing his way over from California in 1978 but I have talked about the Jellyman in the previous chapter and Dennis Sigalos joined him at the Boulevard in 1979.

I had been to America at the beginning of the year to look at Shawn Moran but I didn't think he was ready, even though it was obvious he had massive potential. However, I didn't come home empty handed because I was also very impressed when I saw Sigalos. He was a big friend of Bruce Penhall and, in later life after their speedway careers, the pair of them teamed up to win World Power Boat titles together.

But then, unlike Shawn, he was ready for the ultimate test of racing in Britain and he had two wonderful seasons with us at the Boulevard. He had an average of more than seven from 40 meetings in 1979 and then had the nerve to beat Ivan Mauger to our No. 1 slot in 1980 when he lifted his average by almost two points over 31 matches.

Dennis was a quality rider when he arrived at Hull and he was World class when he left to join Ipswich two years later. His father was an extremely rich man who had a contract to provide food to Disneyland in California. My wife, Dot, and I once stayed at the family's holiday home at Newport Beach which was very exclusive and simply fantastic.

Dennis always had top gear but he didn't behave like a rich kid who had whatever he wanted. He was very professional and was prepared to work hard for success, which is something he wanted very badly.

Unfortunately, he had that American shortcoming of needing someone to blow his nose for him. One night he had ridden in a big individual meeting at Wimbledon which had nothing whatsoever to do with Hull speedway apart from the fact that he'd travelled down in the sponsored car which we provided for him.

I was tucked up in bed at two o'clock in the morning when Dot and I were woken up by a phone call from Dennis to tell me he'd broken down in Peterborough on the way home. He asked me what he should do. I wasn't happy at being woken up, the only thing I know about cars is that they have four wheels so I said: 'How the hell do I know?' and slammed the phone down.

The following week, on the Wednesday morning before we were racing that night, I stayed up until two o'clock and, at the same time as he'd called me, I phoned him and said: 'Dennis, I've just had a call from the printers and the programmes aren't going to be ready for the meeting. What shall I do?'

He replied: 'I don't know anything about programmes.' To which I said: 'Just like what I know about cars. Nothing.' He didn't see the funny side.

But, seriously, Dennis did a brilliant job for us on track. He remains one of the great American riders for me and, apart from broken down cars, he was brilliant to work with and never caused me any real bother. He was a top man and the fans loved his charisma. It rivalled that of Penhall, which is a massive compliment.

Sadly, we had trouble doing a deal with him at the end of the 1980 season, his second with us, and I knew the answer why in two short words. John Berry.

Dennis had been contacted by the Ipswich promoter to go there and that is what happened. I wasn't prepared to get involved in a Dutch auction in a bid to do a deal to keep him and Dennis moved to East Anglia, along with John Cook. We got their Australian star, Billy Sanders, and cash in return. I was very sorry to lose him.

Cook was another of my American recruits but he only stayed for the 1980 season and was another middle order rider. I'll never forget him for just one incident after he joined us, along with Shawn Moran. He really was a flamboyant character who later picked up the nickname of Cowboy at Ipswich.

When we arrived we gave him a sponsored car, with a bike-carrying cradle on the back, but it was emphasised to him that he must not, under any circumstances, drive it until the next day when the insurance kicked in. So what happened? I got a call from him later the same day to say that not only had he driven the car, he'd wrecked it.

I wasn't happy and asked him how. He said he'd gone over 'one of those round things in the road.' I hadn't a clue what he was talking about until he explained that 'I think you call them roundabouts. We don't have them in America.' The upshot was that I had to provide him with another car because the sponsor wasn't too impressed.

John was a good rider but he could be moody and, like all Americans, he wanted everything doing for him. But they are in that kind of profession. He got better when he went to Ipswich. They marketed him well as The Cowboy, a name which stayed with him for the rest of his career which only ended comparatively recently. He based himself in Sweden later and didn't ride much in Britain but he did have a spell at Eastbourne.

I prefer to sign British-based riders these days, as shown by the bulk of the Belle Vue team in 2005. But, overall, I enjoyed my links with the Americans very much indeed.

DENNIS Sigalos, who started his British career at Hull.

JOE Owen, a huge favourite
at Newcastle.

10 – Newcastle: legends were made

I WOULD never want to be called a star-maker because the only people who can do that are the lads themselves who get out on the tracks and ride the bikes.

However, as a long-time promoter, I have given many riders their chance to achieve stardom. Lou Sansom and, more recently, Carl Stonehewer became legends at Workington while, on the other hand, I can look at Kelly Moran and see only a terrible waste of a massive talent.

Sansom and Stonehewer aren't the only two of my signings to become local legends because there are two more and what has made them extra special is they are brothers. Tom and Joe Owen were among my first signings when I opened at Newcastle in 1975 and they were the driving forces behind nine mercurial seasons at Brough Park, even though they were team-mates for only the first two of those success-strewn years in the National League.

We won the championship three times, finished runners-up three times and won the Knockout Cup twice. Heady days, indeed. Tom was with us for the first six years before being badly injured at the start of the seventh. Joe rode for Newcastle in the first two and final two of those glory, glory years before we made the disastrous move up into the British League, which is dealt with in a separate chapter. Incredibly, the pair of them never had an average below the ten-point mark and frequently went over 11.

They became gods on Tyneside while being revered and feared elsewhere. Other promoters hated and loved them at the same time because they often spelled home defeats for their sides while pulling extra fans through their turnstiles. They were sensational every year they were at the club and the North East fans took them to their hearts, even though they were from Ormskirk, in Lancashire.

I couldn't say one was a better rider than the other at Newcastle; you just couldn't split them. I could make out an argument for Joe having the edge because he was younger and had more ambition but only because of that. They were great blokes who came from a lovely family.

They had ridden at Barrow for two seasons before I took them to Newcastle and their averages were in the seven and eight points area when they arrived at Brough Park. They were sound rather than special performers at that time but something clicked for both of them in the North East and they were in double figures from the very start of their careers up there.

They were first and second in the averages, not only at Newcastle but the league in the two years before Joe left. Tom remained to rule the roost for another four years before being injured at the start of 1981. I brought Joe back in 1982 and he led the Diamonds to successive National League championships by topping the averages with a fantastic figure above the 11-point mark.

They were totally contrasting characters. Joe could be a bit volatile while Tom was a little more laid back. It would be wrong to say they didn't get on together but they weren't particularly close. They didn't travel together and the competition between them to be Newcastle's No. 1 was intense, which was great news for me. The differences in their averages was almost always fractional. Tom never wanted to move full-time in the top league although I did use him at Hull when I could. Joe had higher aspirations speedway-wise and I suppose I did keep him down in the second division for a year longer than I should.

I was criticised a great deal by a variety of people for not moving the Owens up into the top league at Hull, because of their success at the secondary level. Joe did go into the top flight eventually but Tom never did, even though he ran a double figure average for six years. So why was it? There are two reasons. Firstly they were good for business, not only for me at Newcastle but for the other tracks in the league. Secondly, in Tom's case, there was the financial angle. He would have been a seven-point man in the British League but, by staying with Newcastle, where he qualified for a testimonial, he made a lot of money, invested it well and now owns one of the largest private plant hire businesses in Lancashire. By staying in the lower league, he secured the future for himself and his family.

I tend to get on my high horse on this subject because this is a free country so what right have other promoters, or some fans, to tell a promising rider to move up? If he wants to, fair enough because it's his decision. But a speedway rider's career is relatively short and if he elects to stay a bigger fish in a smaller pond then that is his right and nobody else's. It's a controversial subject and, more recently, I got the same kind of comments over Simon Stead when he was at Workington. All I can tell these critics is to get off their backs and mine, it's up to a rider how he conducts his career. I'm not going to say that I've never asked a rider to move up because I have. But if he has told me he's happy to stay where he is, I have respected his decision, even if I haven't liked it.

Tom was never the same after suffering a serious leg injury. He finished his career with four seasons at Stoke and I feel he should have retired after the crash. I think it is sad to see a guy struggling for his old glories, especially one who had as much success as Tom. He finished his career with a seven-point average. That was in 1986, the year after Joe's career had been ended by his dreadful crash at Birmingham when riding for Ellesmere Port. But both of them had become part of the fabric of Newcastle speedway long before.

In my view, the Diamonds side of the 1970s was the most successful ever to race at Second Division level. The supporters were brilliant and they would stick with any rider, or promoter for that matter, as long as they felt they were trying. One peculiarity of the Geordies was that, unlike many fans, they didn't like the drama and excitement of a 40-38 home win in those days when league fixtures were run over 13 heats. Normally, the entertainment value wasn't so great if you murdered your opponents but, for them, it was a case of the bigger the win the better. We managed to keep them happy over the years, even though it made for some costly pay nights for the promotion. There's an old saying in speedway that 'Happiness is 40-38' but not with the Geordie fans. People like big wins nowadays because they can help a team to win the aggregate bonus point but they weren't in existence then.

We won a lot of trophies and we were always grateful to the support we received from two local athletics superstars, Brendan Foster and Steve Cram. They would come along to make presentations when we won something big so we saw plenty of them.

I opened Newcastle in 1975 after protracted negotiations with my business partners, Brian Larner and George Graham. Our talks were given an added urgency because we knew that at least two other parties were interested in bringing speedway back to Brough Park stadium after a four-year break.

Mike Parker had been the previous promoter and we meant to be the next. I never discovered the identity of one of the would-be promotions but the other contender was Mrs. Elizabeth Taylor and her son, Kenny, who had run Berwick. We won the battle but George only stayed with us for a short time before Brian and myself bought him out to start nine wonderful years on Tyneside, prior to the financially disastrous ending in 1984.

I appointed Dave Younghusband, the former Halifax star, as general manager and he looked after the team and track. I'm pleased to say we have remained friends over all these years and he visited Belle Vue a few times in 2005 with his son, Ian. Dave also did a round trip to Oxford and Poole with me – and we set off a day early to take in a Showaddywaddy concert so there was plenty of time to remember the good old days at Newcastle.

There were plenty of them from the word go as we finished second to Birmingham in our first season in the National League and then won it by a mile from Ellesmere Port, winning our 17 home matches and losing only three away.

The two signings which made the team in the early days were the Owen boys but we also brought in Brian Havelock, Mike Watkin, Tim Swales and a smattering of Aussies. Tim, who later became chairman of the Promoters' Association, came up to me one day in the first season and asked if it would be possible to have a pay rise. I told him: 'Not a chance.' He said: 'Okay.' And that was the end of it.

I marked the re-birth of the Diamonds by booking Newcastle legend Ivan Mauger to do a series of match races against Jimmy McMillan, who rode for me at Hull. What a night! We had given it the works on the publicity front and it seemed every man and his dog were there or wanted to be there. The traffic jam stretched about three miles from the stadium to the Tyne Bridge and more than 6,000 people paid to watch. Crowds remained good for years and we rewarded them well for their support.

Ivan always told me that Brough Park was a great home track for a World class rider because, of all the British circuits, it was the nearest in shape to Wembley where all the World Finals were ridden in those days.

I even invented two new competitions, the Pairs and the Four Team tournament, to give us something else to aim for and we won them as well. I am pleased to say that, after all these years, the Pairs championship is still held in both the Elite and Premier leagues while the Fours continues to go strong in the Premier.

I was fortunate to have the sponsorship of Lada Cars at Newcastle and Hull, as well as the Wembley Indoor show in which I was involved. I view Lada as the forerunner of big team sponsors coming into speedway and their support over the years was priceless. Journalist Richard Bott was my Publicity Officer at both tracks and we came up with some great Press day ideas. Once we hired a stripper and covered her with balloons, one of which was burst every time a journalist asked a question. She was starkers in a matter of minutes.

I am always on the lookout for an angle to give the media boys because I know they will bite harder if you throw them a line, rather than just call a Press conference. They turned up in droves when when we announced we were signing Tom Owen for life, a move unheard of in speedway. It was a great story but it never worked out that way because I had to transfer list him at the end of the season. Business dictated he had to go because speedway is governed by points' limits and I couldn't fit him in to my plans.

I have a million memories about my time at Newcastle which remains one of the best periods of my career. Aussie Robbie Blackadder was one of our top guys for seven years and, one night, he had a nasty crash at Brough Park when he got his hand mangled in his back wheel. He managed to walk back to the pits unaided. I asked him if he was okay and he replied: ' No, I've lost half a finger.' He put out his hand to show me and I was nearly sick. The track doctor rushed him to hospital in an ambulance and told me to send out the track staff to see if they could find the missing half-digit because there was a slim chance it could be sewn back on. They didn't find it and I reckoned that, as it was a greyhound stadium, one of the dogs would have it for lunch. But not so. Robbie and I were having a walk round the track a few days later when he bent down and picked up his missing finger. It was black. This time I was sick.

Another big Aussie favourite was Rod Hunter, a very bright young man and an excellent rider at this level who also ran a ten-plus average. Jason Crump, who remains in touch with him, told me Rod won the Australian lottery recently and used the winnings to expand his property empire.

I'm not ashamed to admit that I pulled a lot of strokes in my time at Newcastle but, in my view, it is all part and parcel of being a promoter as well as being a reward for knowing the rule book back to front. I once used the rider replacement rule for Robbie Gardner for a whole season and another time I had Tom Owen's average reduced by a big lump after a bad accident so I could fit him into the team under the points limit at the start of a season.

I've talked elsewhere about my last season at Newcastle in 1984 when it all turned sour but I thoroughly enjoyed the other nine years I was up there. I still go on occasions and it's a great testimony to the club that so many people who were there in my era are still around. There's Barry Wallace, who has been the announcer for ever, and a supporter called Mrs. Irene Best who I banned once. She was a Tom Owen fan and she gave me a lot of stick when I let him go. But the ban didn't last for long and she still gives me a kiss when she sees me.

George English senior and his wife, Joan, were a big part of Newcastle speedway over the seasons. Sadly, George passed away a few years ago but George junior is now one of the promoters at Newcastle and can't have many more seasons to do before becoming the club's longest-ever boss. The family will go down in Newcastle folklore. I was happy to be invited to Joan's 70th birthday party in 2005 and recalled the days she played a vital role in my Newcastle days. Dave Younghusband and myself seemed to have more than our share of headaches in those days but Joan worked for a firm that made tablets so we always had a ready-made supply. But, let's face it, what would speedway be without a few headaches?

I always took stick from a section of the Workington crowd when I went back there with Newcastle and there was a major bust-up in 1981 that made all the wrong headlines. It was called a Night of Shame in the local Evening News and Star and, in retrospect, it wasn't a surprise in view of the great competition in what was regarded as a derby match. I had even suspected before the match that there might be problems and had taken the precaution of leaving my Rolls Royce at the Brierli House Hotel, the place where I had taken Ken Dodd for a meal years before, and organising a lift to the track. Little did I know then that I, and the team, would be getting a police escort out of town a few hours later after an outbreak of violence during which my head was cut by a flying stone.

It was a stormy meeting, which the Diamonds won by four points. Rod Hunter was attacked by spectators, beer was thrown over referee John Whittaker and three home riders were injured. It was already a tense match but it really blew up in heat 11 when the Comets were four points ahead. It had to be run three times before Terry Kelly, who had been injured in the crash that caused the first stoppage, won it before collapsing in the pits.

Workington's delight was tempered by referee Whittaker then excluding their rider Guy Wilson, who had finished second, for dangerous riding. He had ridden two laps with a puncture but still managed to keep our rider, Keith Bloxsome, behind him.

Kelly was unable to take his scheduled ride in heat 12 in which Robbie Blackadder and Alan Emerson gave us full points and we went into the final heat just one behind. Wayne Jackson and Wilson jumped out of the gate for the Comets and we looked doomed but Rod Hunter powered under Wilson on the second lap. His bike flew into the fence while he flew over it and he was excluded as the cause of the race being stopped. Punches were thrown as spectators tried to attack Hunter while other fans and track staff battled to keep them off our Aussie star. In the re-run Jackson fell off in a duel with Hunter to be excluded and leave us with a 5-0 heat win and a four-point match victory. Guy Wilson's father told me that Hunter was not responsible for his son's spectacular crash but there was no way I was going to get the message across on the night.

There was a wonderful postscript to the meeting when Wilson turned up in the bar wearing a hospital dressing gown. I didn't see that of course. By then, my team and I were well down the A66. What a night!

IAN Thomas
and son Lyndon
at the first
indoor meeting
at Wembley.

11 – *Speedway crash – with a difference*

I LOST almost everything after Newcastle went down in 1984, including my beautiful house on the edge of the Yorkshire Dales, my hard-earned savings and my pride.

Even more seriously, I feared I was going to lose my life. I received three death threats in telephone calls. They were chilling and very professional. I was extremely frightened by them and I took them seriously. Very seriously indeed.

The Newcastle crash came after the promotion had taken the completely wrong decision to move up from the financial security and almost runaway success of the Second Division into the top flight and we lost £40,000 in a season. That's a lot of money these days but it was a fortune then.

I had put up my house as collateral against the mounting debt to keep the Clydesdale Bank happy and to keep Newcastle speedway alive. It was another two years before the bank forced me to sell our home after I had battled to stay there. It was a dreadful time and it became worse when the phone started to ring.

Even now, I have to be careful what I say because the perpetrator, whoever he was, was never apprehended. The voice said: 'Thomas, you are a xxxxxxx dead man. I'm going to blow your head off.' There was other X-rated stuff I can't repeat here. It shook me up. I don't mind admitting that I was scared and who wouldn't be.

I contacted the village policeman in Menston, who I knew. He took the threats seriously and so did his superiors because Special Branch were brought in. They put a machine on my telephone to record all my calls and an emergency button on my front door. I was instructed to hit it if I felt threatened and I was told the house would be surrounded by police as soon as possible.

I lived on my nerve edges until, finally, Special Branch got a lead on who it was. They went to see him and then came back to tell me it was the right man but that they wouldn't be able to prove anything against him. However, the fact that he'd had his collar felt was the end of it. There were no more calls but I have my own feelings about who was behind it.

I always had doubts in the back of my mind about taking the Diamonds up into the big time. After all, why take a risk with a business that was motoring along quite happily? I'm still not sure why

Wheels and Deals

I and my partner Brian Larner decided to go up and my doubts came to terrible fruition almost from before the moment the first wheel turned in that fateful season.

We brought in a new partner in Robin Stannard because we needed extra financial clout but, by the end of the season, Newcastle had gone bust big style and my friendships with Larner and Stannard had sunk beyond redemption. I've felt ever since that they left me to carry the can and, I have to say, it was a bloody big can.

Newcastle was soon losing £1,000 a week and the bills had to be met. People ask me why I didn't call it a day and pull the plug. But it was a matter of pride that I finished the season, that I fulfilled my commitments and contracts. I'm a stubborn sort of guy and if I get something in my head I'll do it. I knew soon that it wasn't going to work and, even though the trouble only got deeper and deeper, I couldn't countenance the kind of adverse publicity it would give speedway as a whole if a top-flight club folded.

I put up my beautiful house in Menston, near Ilkley Moor, as collateral when the bad times started to roll. The bank wanted more money injecting and I had to use the house because I didn't have the liquid cash they wanted. It was a bad, bad time. My health suffered, my wife and family suffered and, but for their support and escaping onto the golf course, I could so easily have gone under.

Things were bad enough, believe me, but they could have been even worse. I felt sorry for myself but I felt even worse for my wife, Dot, and son Lyndon. I felt very guilty about what I put them through. They were sticky times and Dot deserved a medal for sticking with me. To lose your house must be one of the most awful things that can happen to you and to have no money isn't nice. Neither is not having a job, especially when it has been one that you have loved doing for almost 15 years. It was the low point and I said to the family: 'This is where and when we start again.' And we did.

As I've said, I could have gone under for good but thankfully, I'm made of sterner stuff than that and I set about rebuilding our lives. I developed my fascination for magic and saw the possibilities it offered me as an alternative career and source of income.

Also, I still had my experience as a promoter to fall back on, even though my latest experience hadn't been a happy one. I used it to help one of my former riders, Graham Drury, launch indoor speedway on ice at Telford, in 1986, and to take it around Europe and the Middle East. Telford is now established as the longest running indoor speedway meeting in the world.

We had been forced to leave the family home at the insistence of the bank, who I will never use again, and moved into a smaller property nearby. We were absolutely skint but I was determined that I would be back and that I would restore the family fortunes. My circumstances gradually turned full circle and, in November, 1992 I pushed open the front door of our lovely new home which was paid for and, to my intense satisfaction, it was next door to the one I had been forced to leave.

It had been my dream to go back when I left and I managed to get an option on a plot of land adjoining where we had been living. It was a moving moment when we returned to 'our road' in Menston. I like to think of myself as a hard-bitten, tough Yorkshireman but, on that occasion, I am not ashamed to admit that I wept openly. I'd told Dot that we wouldn't attempt to go back there until we could afford it without taking a mortgage and without owing money to anyone. And that is what happened.

I had scratched, scraped and battled to get back on my feet. Walking through that door meant I'd done it. I counted myself a lucky man. After all, I'd tasted the high life at the top before crashing to the bottom. Not everyone is fortunate enough to rise again to the top but I did it. Yes, I was proud of what I'd done but it didn't stop me thanking my lucky stars, either.

My love for golf was a great crutch through my blackest days. I found out who my real friends were and they took me out to get me away from my problems for a few hours. My enforced new career in magic, indoor speedway and ice shows even paid the rich dividend of allowing me to play at exotic locations throughout the Middle East and the West Indies.

I gradually picked up the old traces after recovering from the biggest mistake of my life of going into the big-time with Newcastle. The Diamonds had been the top dogs in the old National League, winning all the top trophies between the late 1970's and 1983. We had cleaned up the top awards in 1982 and landed the championship and team trophies again in 1983. The pressure to take on the British League big boys grew to the point where it couldn't be resisted, whatever my misgivings.

We did market research and that seemed to indicate that the people of Tyneside wanted it. Our big mistake showed up later. Where we went wrong was that we canvassed only our regular fans. We didn't get out on the streets and talk to the Newcastle public and that was crucial because we needed new fans to cover the higher costs of top speedway.

Wheels and Deals

We knew there was an element of a gamble in meeting the higher costs and that's why Stannard came on board because we needed an injection of capital.

Larner and myself agreed to sell a third share in Newcastle to Stannard, a businessman from York who sponsored our top rider, Joe Owen. There were problems even before Newcastle started life in the First Division. The first cheque due from Stannard bounced, although it was honoured later. But the final two thirds due from him was never paid. Another problem was that the crowds never lived up to expectations, even though we won our first two away matches. Some people claimed that the team wasn't strong enough but those two victories answered that so I didn't accept that criticism. Those successes were at Coventry and Wolverhampton.

When we started to lose money I agreed to take a charge on my house. I wanted Larner to make the same commitment with his house but he said his wife wouldn't agree to it. He gave me assurances that it wouldn't be a problem if things got really bad and like an idiot I believed him. They did get really bad. I woke every Monday on the morning of our race night knowing that at least another £1,000 would be going down the pan. That was a lot of money in those days and still is. It was a horrible feeling. These days I look out of the window on race day hoping the weather will be fine. In those days I was praying it would be bad so we could have a rain-off.

Yes, I know that I should have pulled the plug halfway through the season but what would that have done for speedway's reputation? You lived in the hope that things would improve and that, if they didn't, your partners would stand their corners. It's wrong that a track should close in mid-season. I'm not trying to sound righteous but even though I knew I couldn't turn it round in that season, I couldn't close down. I remember that Hackney later failed to finish a season and it's terrible for speedway when that happens.

There is bound to be friction in a situation like we had that year at Brough Park and, towards the end of the season, Larner even stopped coming to the meetings. To be fair to Stannard, at least he put in an appearance.

I suppose Newcastle lost £40,000 in running costs over the year but the overall loss was much higher due to having to buy riders to move up into the British League. Some of those debts were paid off by selling riders through the British Speedway Promoters' Association with the most substantial fee the £17,000 for the transfer of Joe Owen to Ellesmere Port. We also sold Eddie Ingells to Belle Vue.

I am not suggesting it was a good time for Larner and Stannard either but, for one reason or another, they didn't come up with the promised payments. I was the real big loser. It can be argued that they did contribute because they would have owned a third each of the Joe Owen and Ingells contracts but we never saw a penny of that money because it was paid into the BSPA by the purchasing clubs and used by them to pay debts. But while I paid out other cash, they never contributed a penny.

My bitterness towards Larner and Stannard remains and will do so for the rest of my life. I hired private investigators and lawyers to try to recover the money I was owed for fulfilling Newcastle's obligations. I never saw any of it. I was left to carry the can. I lost my house, which the bank forced me to sell, because two people in the Newcastle promotion did not stand their corners. I can substantiate that to the letter. But every one of Newcastle's debts were paid and that included one guy, who shall remain nameless, who received his money many years later when I could afford it. It wasn't a speedway debt as such and only a third of it was my liability but I paid the lot.

It was the end of a brilliant friendship with Larner and wrecked a very successful business partnership. We had met in 1970 and we were great pals for years. We were a good partnership with me the miserable you know what while he was the extrovert. There had never been any hassle until 1984. Brian bought out Wally Mawdsley, who had opened Hull with me in 1971. I was the major shareholder, 60-40, while Wally was there and then I went 50-50 with Brian. Later we reopened Newcastle with George Graham, who we bought out soon afterwards.

Brian and I got up to some crazy stunts. We both liked a bet and to put some spice into the weekly trips to Newcastle, which went on for ten years, we occasionally took turns to hitchhike from Wetherby or Scotch Corner to Newcastle. The other would drive up after giving the hitcher a start and the first to arrive at the track would win a bet.

Barmy? Yes. But we never missed a meeting and it was a laugh. I once saw Brian soaked to the skin in a lay-by with his thumb in the air. I gave him a wave. It wasn't in the rules to pick him up. We'd even bet on the number of bridges on a stretch of motorway.

Brian nailed Barry Briggs and me with a great stunt in 1977 when Briggo was riding for us at Hull. We got a call from the police to say Larner had been arrested and needed someone to bail him out. When we got to the police station, the sergeant said that Brian had tried to hit one of his officers and then tried to hang himself with his braces. We fell for it a treat but Brian had set up the whole thing.

Wheels and Deals

Sadly, those happy days ended in such bitterness. None of us have spoken for years. And we never will.

I've only seen Stannard once since 1984 and that was at an auction selling repossessed houses and that was one time too many. He was sitting behind me. I had gone to buy a property for investment purposes and when I failed to get it I left. I walked past him on the way and I leaned over and said: "Stannard, you're a xxxxx." He looked at the floor and never said a word.

I feel that Larner let me down in an even bigger way because we'd had such a good partnership for so many years. I've only seen him once since that fateful season. That was in the bar at Coventry speedway where he looked at me and waved. I just walked away. I've got a long memory and I believe that what goes around comes around. I know I'm wrong to say this but I'm delighted to have heard that he hasn't done too well since the Newcastle debacle.

Life is fine again now. I'm very happy running a great club at Belle Vue, business is good and the family are now in a better position than we were before the Newcastle drama happened. I'm talking about every aspect of my life here but it is especially important to me that I'm living in a beautiful house in the village where I was born. It's the village and the house where I want to die.

But that, hopefully, will be in my own good time and not as the result of a death threat!

12 – A magic recovery

I HAVE been incredibly lucky that the two main strands of my working life, speedway and magic, have also been my hobbies. How many people can honestly say that they absolutely love what they do for a living?

Magic was purely a hobby until I hit financial problems when Newcastle closed down in 1984. Then, suddenly, I was forced to look urgently for another source of income and, quite by accident, I turned to magic thanks to another great love of my life, golf.

I'd always been interested in the magic and, around 1980, I started to read books about it before moving on to teach myself a few illusions. I was soon hooked on it and my repertoire grew, even though I never viewed it as anything more than a bit of fun for a long time. When I played golf I would take a few bits and bobs in my pocket and try to entertain or baffle my playing partners when we adjourned to the 19th hole afterwards.

I am a member at the Hawksworth club, near my home, and I went to play in a pro-am at Cleckheaton. It was late in the year and I was partnered with my club pro against a couple from Keighley. I did a couple of tricks over a pint afterwards and the guy in the Keighley team who wasn't the pro turned out to be the club's social secretary.

He asked me if I would go to their Christmas dinner party and do some close-up magic at the tables. I knew I wasn't up to a professional standard in any way, shape or form and I rejected the invitation. Then he said would I do it if he gave me £150 cash. I said: 'Yes, it's not a problem.'

Come the day I was a bag of nerves. I got a pal to drive me up to Keighley and, when I got there, I went to the bar and had a double whisky. That was totally unprofessional to start with and I certainly wouldn't do it these days. Firstly, I can't risk being drunk when I am working and, secondly, I don't want to breathe alcohol over people, especially when they are having a meal. Anyway, I got on with the show round the tables and, to my surprise, it went down very well. I thought: 'I can give this a go on a professional basis.'

I knew I wasn't ready at that point but I got my head down and practised and practised for at least another six months. I've always been able to think on my feet, a case of bull baffling brain, so I knew I could handle the patter and when I'd enough tricks in place I started to market myself. Touch wood, I've never looked back and I've done all kinds of jobs in many countries. I've been billed as Ian Thomas: International Magician and I guess that's right when you look at the places I've been.

York at six o'clock in the morning hardly comes in that category but that was the scene of one of my most unusual jobs. I was booked by The Big Breakfast programme to do a live TV show – at a set of traffic lights in the city. A guy called to ask if I was available for a job which required me to wear a white tuxedo at 6.45 in the morning. I thought it was one of my mates winding me up.

They were always looking for different stories and their researchers had discovered some traffic lights which stayed on red for longer than they were on green. They were causing rush hour jams so they asked me if I would go along and entertain motorists while they were sitting in the queue. I said I was game for it and we did a deal.

So I turned up, complete with my white tuxedo which brought me some whistles from a group of builders who walked past. The presenter told me that when a car pulled up at the lights, he would knock on the passenger's window and, if it was opened, he would ask if they wanted to see some close-up magic while they were sitting there. If they agreed, I had to dive in. I would have my back to the lights so the presenter said he would kick me on the ankle when they changed so I'd know when to finish.

So off I go, my first live network TV gig. And what happens with the first car that pulls up? The presenter leaps in, down goes the window and he's confronted by a Chinese girl who can't speak a word of English. I asked her to pick a card but she just smiled at me so I handed one over to her. It wasn't magic but I just talked until the lights changed. The next car was okay and the trick worked. The TV people were happy and I got paid so I was happy.

I've also done a couple of Christmas trips to Lapland. The first one was a day out from Gatwick and the plane was full of kids going to see Santa. I had to entertain them on the way out while caricaturist Ray Allen, who I use a lot in my entertainment agency, did drawings for the youngsters. We'd driven down overnight from a Christmas party in Skipton and were ready for a kip by the time we arrived in Lapland. But Thomsons, the organisers, included us in the whole trip and kitted us out with the right clothing because it was about 20 degrees below.

We rode around on a skidoo and then went on a half-hour forest drive to see Santa. We stopped en route to see some dancing elves and we were given a drink, obviously non alcoholic. Ray and myself must have looked a bit strange in this party because two of the girls dressed up as elves came up and asked us if we were homosexuals. We said indignantly that we weren't and asked them if they were Lesbians. Some Christmas spirit, eh?

We arrived at Santa's village, saw the husky dogs, went sledging and then, like a couple idiots, we queued up for half an hour for a private audience with Father Christmas. When we went in, he just looked up and said: 'Hello boys. I remember visiting you when you were seven.' What a brilliant line. We got back to the airport for the flight home and went to the gents before boarding. Another bloke came in and asked us if we were working. We told him why we were there and asked him the same question. He stood there at the trough and replied: 'Yes, I'm Father Christmas.' It's not everyone who has had a pee with Santa. He was on the way home because he did the job on a week-on week-off basis. Ray said: 'You've ruined my day.' To which Santa replied: 'As long as you don't ruin it for all those kids!' The guy was perfect for the job.

My second trip was for a Cosmos day trip. I had to be at Gatwick at 3.30 in the morning and when I arrived I was told that as, part of my performance, I'd have to interact with a reindeer. A real one. I hadn't had too much experience of reindeer, living near Bradford, and this thing was about twice my size but I managed. The woman telling me what to do struck me as a bit of a bitch so I thought it might help my day if I established a rapport with her. I asked her if I could read her mind and she said: 'If you must.' I said: 'Hey, it's not compulsory' and walked away. I was tempted to go home but that wouldn't have been professional so I went, inter-acted with a reindeer and, while it wasn't as enjoyable as the Thomson trip, it didn't turn into a bad day.

I've done magic at a corporate function on the London Eye, which was very interesting, and have performed at many military venues and football clubs. I also performed my Man In The Iron Mask routine at Silverstone when there were 250,000 people watching. I've done Headingley Cricket Club, in Leeds, at an end-of-run party for the cast of the Touch Of Frost TV series. I went up to David Jason to do magic for him and he was absolutely delightful. In all, I've done 17 trips to the Middle East as well as Bermuda, the Caribbean, Tenerife and all over Europe.

One thing I won't do is mix speedway with magic although I had to make an exception last season when BBC TV came to do a piece at Belle Vue. Their reporter, Dan Walker, phoned and asked me if I'd do a live card trick. I tried to duck out by saying I'd got no props with me but he said he'd buy a pack of cards on the way to the track so I was cornered. But it went off fine and, suitably, I got him to pull the Ace of Clubs out of the pack while people all over the North West of England watched. That's what I call media exposure. It was good for Belle Vue and it was good for my CV, as well.

I once did a British Week in Jordan which was a great experience. I went out with a three-piece jazz band fronted by a singer called Gary Williams who has done well for himself since. John Inman was out there with Ruth Madoc who was a delightful lady. We were put up in a nice hotel in Ammann and I thought I was doing okay until the Jordanian agent asked me when I was going to do some real magic. I took that to mean he thought I was crap. He said the last magician had taken them into the desert and brought back to life 500 animals that had been dead for 10,000 years. I said: 'Tell you what, book him next time.'

I've appeared twice in front of Jordanian royalty. Once was for two princes at a party hosted by British Airways and they called my wife Ma'am which made her day. One of them was fascinated by levitation and he asked me if I could do it for him. It's not my area of magic because I do close-up but, by coincidence, I had a trick where I hold a card, get the punter to put a match on it and it floats. I thought this was a great chance to win some Brownie points in high places so I said: 'Would you like to come over to the corner, Your Highness.'

I did the trick and he was knocked out by it. So I asked him if he would like me to show him how to do it which I did. You would have thought I'd given him the moon when he did it.

Another night I was performing on a TV show but first a party of us had been invited by the British Ambassador to have lunch at his residence. He told me that a Jordanian princess, complete with armed guards, would be coming to watch a play starring Ruth Madoc and John Inman but, first, I was to do some magic while a caricaturist stood behind me and drew her. She was the most beautiful lady but I discovered the real meaning of the word pressure when I was trying to perform surrounded by two guys carrying machine guns. Looking at them, I'd no doubt they wouldn't have thought once, never mind twice, about using them. But it was an absolutely brilliant trip.

Another time I was booked for a week in Qatar in the Middle East at the most beautiful venue I've been to anywhere in the world. It was called the Aldana Club and it was staging an ATP tennis tournament, with all the top blokes like Tim Henman taking part. I went to watch a match before a show, wearing my dinner suit, and I was captivated. I'd never liked tennis until then but I do now after watching that.

I hadn't been told by the agent but I had also been booked to appear at a theme park called Aladdin's Kingdom. It was Ladies' Day, one of two days a week when only women and children were admitted. If you are found in there without the right credentials you are nicked. As an entertainer I was okay, or so I thought. I had been worried about how I would manage to do close-up magic in a theme park and those fears were realised when I was shown into a big outdoor theatre containing an audience of about 400 people.

I was told to entertain them for 20 minutes but my act has to be performed right under their noses. I told him I couldn't do it for 400 people at once but he just told me that I had to. I wasn't helped by the fact that the women were wearing yashmaks so I couldn't see the reactions on their faces and I suspected that many, or most, of them couldn't speak English. Talk about being up a fig tree! An Egyptian band was due on after me and, almost as soon as I had tried to get my act going, the drummer came out behind me and started to practise. I knew even before he struck up that my act was going to die on its feet so a rampant Egyptian drummer banging away behind me was all I needed.

I turned round, walked over to the offending musician, and said: 'Give me an xxxxing chance mate, I'm dying here.' He cleared off and left me to my fate for the longest 20 minutes of my life. The audience couldn't see the tricks or understand what I was saying. When I asked a lady to pick a card there was no response so I had to pick one for her and that rather defeated the object of the exercise.

I kept trying to do tricks but I also resorted to Plan Two which is when you allow bull to baffle brain and talk a lot. I told them about the night my act died in the Sunderland Empire and thought about the comedians who had told me about the times their acts had fallen flat. I was sure they had never had a night like this. My wife, Dot, was acting as timekeeper and I bet you could almost touch my relief when, finally, she signalled the end of my misery. But that relief was nothing compared with the shock I received as I took my bow. I got a standing ovation. I can only assume they were being polite but the boss seemed happy and it made me realise the importance of the saying 'The show must go on.' That remains one of my great beliefs.

I've died much nearer home than Qatar. It was in a pub in Scunthorpe called Henry Afrika's. An agent rang me one lunchtime, said a comedian had let him down and would I do a 20-minute stand-up spot. I don't like stand-up jobs, as I have explained, but I accepted and decided to take my son, Lyndon, to help with the Unrideable Bike and Electric Chair acts which I also did. We were booked for 7.45 and we arrived an hour early to be greeted by two bouncers who were built like brick outhouses. I didn't like the look of the place at all and I was less impressed when one of them asked: 'Are you the turn?' I looked up at him and said: 'I'm anything you want.' He said: 'You're on at 11.' I didn't dare mention we'd been booked for more three hours earlier. We didn't quite get booed off but I decided the only reason was that Scunthorpe United had drawn with Leeds that afternoon in the FA Cup and everyone in the town was happy.

I was booked once to perform at a funeral by a lady in Hull whose husband had died. I asked her why she wanted a magician at a wake. She said she might not need me but that it wasn't a very close family and she was worried the two sides might not get on very well. I did a little bit of magic but really it went off very well.

It's amazing how many times you are asked the same question when you are close to people while you are performing. Mainly you can't be rude to people but you don't want to give anything anyway. They say: 'How do you do that?' I have two stock answers: 'Very well, I thought,' or 'With great difficulty.' I get a lot of questions and comments because every time I go to a fresh table, it's like having a fresh audience. Others say: 'I know how you did that.' My reply is: 'Well you can earn a living as a magician as well.' Occasionally I'm asked to do a trick again and I say: 'I'd love to but miracles don't happen twice.'

I get the occasional clever dick, usually a bloke, so I always need the right kind of put-down which will be effective without giving offence. If anyone is rude I usually say: 'I don't normally do children's magic but for you I'll make an exception.' That usually brings the rest of the audience onto his back and I'm off the hook.

But the good jobs I attract outweigh the bad ones and the market is sheer magic at the moment. The corporate section is booming. We do hundreds of weddings, there are stacks of bookings for blue chip companies and, all the time, it's amazing how many speedway fans I meet in the course of a year. I don't know if that's because I've got to know so many people over the years or because the sport is becoming more popular and people are seeing me on TV. Perhaps it's a bit of each.

I've got my own entertainment agency, the Ian Thomas Organisation, and the busiest act is Ray Allen, the caricaturist who has a residency at Manchester City Football Club's home games. Not for the first time last year, I got a booking for Ray and it was only at the last minute we discovered they were expecting the ventriloquist with his dummy, Lord Charles. Heaven knows what would have happened if he had turned up.

As I said, I'm lucky to make a living through the two things I like best but I'm not the first promoter to say that. Rye House promoter Len Silver said that about his two passions of speedway and skiing. I'm not the best magician in the world, but I can think on my feet and get by. And, if you do want to see the best in the world, and happen to be in Las Vegas, go to see Lance Burton at the Monte Carlo Hotel and tell him Ian Thomas sent you.

FULL of beans ... England team managers Ian Thomas a nd Eric Boocock on their special diet!

13 – 1980: the Grand Slam season

IT was September 20, 1980 and my nerve ends were stretched to screaming point. It was the night before the World Team Cup final and I was poised to create speedway history by becoming the first national team manager to achieve the Grand Slam of all three championships.

Dave Jessup and Peter Collins had already won the World Pairs in Krkso, Yugoslavia (now Slovenia) in the June and Michael Lee had lifted the individual crown in Gothenburg a fortnight earlier. Now I was in a hotel bar in Wroclaw, Poland, with England coach Eric Boocock trying to relax and counting down the hours to our date with destiny.

We had battled through a troubled year of constant carping and criticism from fellow promoters and sections of the media about the way we had done the job. We had taken it all, done it our way and were poised for the ultimate triumph. But if we thought we were entitled to worry about the last hurdle in peace, we were wrong.

I've mentioned before that a former England team manager and prominent promoter came over and told us we'd been crap at the job. He told us we'd selected the wrong team. I've never divulged before who it was but our arch critic, and not the only one I hasten to add, was senior British promoter Reg Fearman. I was drinking wine at the time and I was so incensed that he had chosen this moment to have a go that I could easily have whacked him over the head with the bottle. Wine was only about £1 a bottle in Poland in those days but I still didn't think it was worth wasting it over his head.

He accused us of not being able to pick a team but there was no doubt he certainly knew how to pick his time to have a go. He had been a decent England team manager, having taken the side to Australia, and I feel his problem was he probably resented the success that Booey and I had enjoyed. He obviously thought we wouldn't win and wanted to make the point in advance. I saw him in the aftermath of the meeting, when we had won and I had created my own piece of history. I said simply: 'You were wrong.' I left it at that and Reg made no reply but, I have to say, those three words gave me a great deal of pleasure. He didn't seem happy England had won.

The pair of us went out of speedway and it was a number of years before I saw him again at a Veteran Dirt Track Riders' dinner. I went up to him and said: 'Reg, I used to bloody hate you as a person. But you were a brilliant speedway promoter.'

Wheels and Deals

Len Silver wasn't the greatest fan of the way I did the England job, either, and he followed me into the position when I was forced to stand down at the end of the 1980 season following a car crash. That's a story on its own. I had asked for a year off to recover from the accident but the Promoters' Association refused and called a big Press conference in London to announce Len's appointment. I was very brassed off about the way I had been rejected. I felt I deserved better after what had been achieved so I went along and upstaged the show.

Booey and myself were there to receive International Motor Federation scrolls from the Speedway Control Board marking our achievements. I've got the one for winning the World Pairs title while Eric has the one for the Team championship and money couldn't buy mine off me. It's hanging on the wall in my office at home. The Control Board normally keep the FIM scrolls but we were given them because of our great partnership in charge. The presentation was to be followed by the big announcement that I wasn't carrying on and that Len was the new England manager. So when I revealed that I was going out of the job, I then wrecked all the planning by announcing Len was taking over. Boy, was I popular for that.

Unfortunately, Reg and Len weren't the only promoters who didn't give us a great deal of support and we learned to use their comments to our advantage at team talks. Reg, unwittingly, played his part in England winning the World Team Cup. We thought the Americans were our only real opposition in the final, which proved correct, and we exploited the fact that him and others didn't think we were good enough. We gave it to the lads hard and fast in the team talk about what their own promoters thought about their chances and that really helped to fire them up.

I think Len is brilliant now and there is a rich irony about what I've said about Reg Fearman. That came after Belle Vue had lost to Coventry in the Elite League play-off final last October when he sent me a lovely e-mail wishing the Aces all the best for the future and complimenting the new promotion on turning things round at Kirkmanshulme Lane. Thanks Reg, it was much appreciated and I guess it proves the old saying that time is a great healer. The fact that we're all a bit older now makes a difference as well.

When Eric and I took over the England job we decided that we'd look like a team. International sides often looked a bunch of scruffs so we made our lads wear blazers with England badges and a tie – although that wasn't always so easy as you will read later in the book. The Americans in particular extracted the you-know-what out of the lads and they didn't like it. They had a saying that 'It takes more than a badge' and laughed at us.

But I remember going to a function the night before the World Pairs final. We looked like a team and we were a team while some of the others looked like Rag, Tag and Bobtail. I'm positive it helped us psychologically. We used the American jibe to our advantage because we turned their comment into our rallying call and, after we'd won the Team Cup, we threw it back in their faces. When we went out on parade to collect our medals we shouted: 'It takes more than a blankety badge!'

They had looked a beaten side even before the final. They looked very nervous, apart from Bruce Penhall who was flamboyant and charismatic then and still is now. I'd never imagine that a team of Americans would lose their cool but perhaps our image, our look and our attitude psyched them out on the day.

One thing that did come out and shouldn't have done was the pipe belonging to that lovely man, the late John Scott, who was the English team manager of the Americans. On the flight out to Warsaw, en route to Wroclaw, John had put his jacket on the back of his seat and gone to sleep. His pipe was sticking out of the pocket. Well, we had nothing much else to do so we borrowed it. One of the lads had some contraceptives so we knocked out the tobacco, inserted a contraceptive, and replaced the tobacco on top. We knew he couldn't smoke on the aircraft but we also knew he would light up at the earliest opportunity after we had landed. We stuck close to him until he did and, I have to say, you have never smelled anything like it in your life. He may have suspected we did it but he never said anything.

I have made a lot of how we tried to psyche out the opposition in various ways, but I must stress England had a lot of World class riders to choose from at that time and, without that quality and strength in depth, we couldn't have won anything. I also feel the amount of talent we had at our disposal contributed to the amount of criticism we attracted, because there were so many options and everyone had their own ideas of what was our strongest side. All I can say is that we must have made the right decisions because we won all the trophies and that is the perfect answer to everyone.

Chris Morton was joint top scorer with Michael Lee in the Team Cup final, each of them scoring 11 points. I gave Mort his first England cap in a Test match earlier in the season against America at Wimbledon. It ended in a 54-54 draw and was the best speedway meeting I've seen in my life. People say the 1982 World Final at Wembley was the best but I was there as well and stick by my view that the Wimbledon Test was better. Morton was dynamite at Wimbledon and was England's top scorer with 12 but he was the same every time he put on an international race jacket. He was brilliant and words can't describe his performance in the Team Cup Final. It was definitely beyond the call of duty.

We were hammered for picking both Peter Collins and Dave Jessup for the Pairs Final. It's not being disrespectful to describe PC as a poor gater while Jessup was on fire. So we confounded convention by giving Collins the best gates on the inside and left Jessup to look after himself off the outside gates. It worked like a charm because they finished first and second in their first five races and dropped a solitary point in the last. Again the critics were silenced and in some style, as well.

We were often accused of a northern bias in our selections and I know we did pick a lot of northern based riders. There were others like Michael Lee, John Davis, Malcolm Simmons, Gordon Kennett and John Louis to consider as well as Kenny Carter and Chris Morton. But we made our decision and we won it.

I've taken a few gambles in my speedway career and not all of them have come off. But that one did and it remains one of the highlights of my career. That's why I'm so proud of that scroll on my wall at home. It was an unbelievable weekend because there were riders like Ivan Mauger and Ole Olsen taking part. Also, after practice I was carted off by two big guys in a big black Mercedes into the mountains. I thought I'd been kidnapped. We finished up in a vineyard at a function for FIM officials. I got stoned and had to sober up for the pre-meeting reception in the evening. Some manager, eh? Krsko is in Slovenia now and I've promised myself that I'll go back there one day to re-live a marvellous weekend.

Jessup was a southern-based rider who was brilliant for me, both in the Pairs and Team Cup. I still see him regularly when I go to Arena-Essex and he still winds me up about the fact that I left him behind in Poland after the Team Cup victory. He had lost his passport and I had to get back for a meeting at Newcastle but he still tells everyone in shouting distance that this is the England manager who left him stranded. I tell him he shouldn't have lost his passport although it emerged he'd had it stolen.

Many people felt that John Davis, known as Mavis, was something of a poser. But I always used to book him a lot at Newcastle. He was flamboyant and I felt he was good for speedway. He projected himself and the sport well and made our seven-man Test team but just missed out on a place in the World Team Cup Final. I dropped Kenny Carter to make John reserve and when he moaned about it I just told him: 'Think yourself lucky. Kenny isn't even here.' And, to his great credit, he did. He didn't get a ride but he was an integral part of the team because he mucked in and helped.

I finished my season in charge of the England team as a Grand Slam record breaker, but those heady moments in September were a far cry from the start of my tenure. My reign was brief and smattered with such constant aggravation that, since 1980, I have never criticised another national team manager and I never will. I know at first hand what they have to go through.

I've been there, taken more stick than you would ever imagine and, thankfully, I am too old to go down that road again. When I look back to 25 years ago, I still find it hard to believe I lasted the season in view of all the criticism and lack of co-operation I suffered. I wrote a book in 1980, with journalist Richard Bott, called Speedway Grand Slam and I remember saying, even in the reflected glow of massive success, just how much unnecessary aggravation myself and Booey had suffered.

We even resigned before we had taken charge of our first meeting. One or two promoters were unhappy when we insisted on the freedom to select whoever we wanted but, reluctantly, they agreed. Then, when we named our side for our first two Test matches against America, they went back on their word. We had picked Kenny Carter, of Halifax, as one of the reserves but we were told we'd have to withdraw him because Halifax were a Saturday night track and they had a fixture clash with the second Test at Cradley Heath.

We resigned but finally accepted the compromise of having a free hand for World Championship meetings if we avoided clashes with club fixtures for Test matches. That didn't prevent a further bust-up with Halifax promoter Eric Boothroyd when we picked Carter as reserve for the Inter-Continental Final of the World Team Cup, as it was called then. My Hull team were riding against Halifax on the same night and he felt Carter had been selected at reserve just to stop him riding in the club match.

Hull were without Dennis Sigalos, who was riding for America, but I had taken the precaution of telling the the Promoters' Association that I was prepared to switch the date of the match and that is what finally happened.

Despite everything, I would have carried on at the end of that year but for the car accident, but I've no desire to do it again now. No way.

14 – Lee: a natural talent, but ...

MICHAEL Lee, along with Kelly Moran, is one of the biggest and most tragic wastes of talent that speedway has ever seen.

I never got very close to Michael and never had a great deal to do with him, other than in 1980 when I was the England team manager and he won the World individual and Team Cup titles in a momentous season. But I observed him as an opposing promoter and team manager for years and feel that here was a man who had the World at his feet and kicked it into touch.

Michael talked openly in the excellent Backtrack magazine last year about his drug problem and his time in prison. He didn't show any remorse for being a drug dealer which I found very sad. But I was delighted to read that he is drug free these days and leading a happy, contented life. Maybe, if he had never been involved with drugs, he could be rich, happy and contented.

He wasn't easy to handle in the Grand Slam year. England had started that season with a Test series against America and, afterwards, I had great reservations about using Michael. His form wasn't particularly good and both Eric Boocock, the England coach, and myself felt he was doing too much too soon after a bad back injury.

He looked jaded and, at that time of the season, Michael's attitude wasn't what we would have wanted but, I have to say, once we got down to business in the World Team Cup, he had changed and his dedication to the cause surprised me. I still have vivid memories of a race in the final in Poland when he missed the gate by yards and, in that class of competition, I feared a last place. But he stormed under everyone on the first two bends to keep us on track with a brilliant victory.

Michael was a rider who could produce the goods when it mattered, as he proved so emphatically in the World Final in Gothenburg. Perhaps his problem was that, on too many occasions, speedway didn't matter enough for him and, too often, he had off-track distractions which mattered more. He was his own worst enemy, the George Best of speedway. Both were wayward stars and, probably, both lacked the necessary degree of backing to help them cope with the trappings and pressure of fame and success.

As I've mentioned elsewhere in the book, I brought in a dress code because I wanted England to look like a team instead of a bunch of scruffs. That included wearing a blazer and tie and, initially, Michael was having none of that. He seemed to like being seen as a rebel but Eric Boocock and myself put a lot of pressure on him to conform. We would have looked stupid with one rider different from the rest and, eventually, he agreed reluctantly to wear a blazer along with the other boys.

During the season we persuaded the Promoters' Association to send us to a Team Cup round by private jet with the bikes going overland. But Michael rebelled again and this time we couldn't shift him so he went on his own by road and sea. Journalist Richard Bott took his place on the plane.

Everything was very scarce in Poland in 1980 when we won the Team Cup in Wroclaw but, to their credit, the Polish Federation put on a superb banquet for all the officials and riders. Belle Vue's Jack Fearnley was the BSPA President at the time and obviously he was very proud as he took his seat at the top table with all the other dignitaries. Eric, who worked for him running the Aces, and myself were feeling quite pleased with ourselves as well as the function got under way.

Then, suddenly, a loud voice came from the back of the room singing – if you could call it singing – Day-oh, Day-oh. We couldn't see who it was but Eric and I looked at each other. Jack Fearnley looked down at us. Eric and I said at the same time: 'It's Lee.' Something had to be done, both from England's perspective and in respect to the Polish authorities who deserved better for their efforts in laying on the banquet.

Eric and I got up from the table, left the room and found a hotel security guard. We gave him £20 in sterling, which was an absolute fortune for a Pole in those days. Michael was still doing his Day-oh routine and we asked the guard, through an interpreter, if he would take him to his room and keep him there until the function was over. That's what happened. The guard stood outside the door and made sure that Michael stayed inside and that no-one else got in.

Why did he start behaving in a manner that would embarrass the new World Team champions and his country? What made him do it? I can't answer those questions but there must have been a reason. And, whatever it was, it certainly seemed to have one hell of an effect on him.

I'll never forget our first encounter back in the 1970s. He was only a kid and was riding for Boston in a meeting at Newcastle. The trackstaff had taken the bikes out for the parade but, for some reason,

Michael's bike had been moved. I don't know who had done it or why but it was in the wrong place. Michael was accompanied by his dad, Andy, and I asked for the machine to be returned to the correct place. They refused so I started to move it myself but, unfortunately, it fell over. Andy seemed to think I'd thrown it down on purpose, which wasn't the case, and he took a swing at me. He's a big guy and, luckily for me, he missed. I quickly explained that I'd tripped on the white line kerb on the inside of the track.

I booked Michael several times over the five years that I was involved in the Wembley indoor meetings and, in that period, he was the only rider who ever failed to turn up. He never even called to say he wasn't coming, nor did he ring afterwards to explain his absence but John Davis didn't mind because he was a reserve and took his place.

I remember Michael riding for King's Lynn at Hull and he was due to race in Germany the following day. But he went out on the town with Kelly Moran after the meeting and never made Germany so it was an expensive night out.

Michael achieved the ultimate in speedway by winning the World title and no-one can ever take that away from him. But I honestly believe that he could have done so much more in his career and that is why I feel sad that he wasted his talent because life is short and you only get one chance.

I don't put him in the top echelon of speedway riders but he was certainly a brilliant racer. I wouldn't include him in the same category as the likes of Ivan Mauger, Barry Briggs and Jason Crump who have all ridden for me over the years. That doesn't mean other judges wouldn't describe him as the finest rider they had ever seen and they include John Berry, another former England team boss.

AMERICAN stunt rider
Doug Democos

15 – Going indoors at Wembley

I'VE had my share of bright ideas over the years but indoor speedway at Wembley, which was such a success for five years, wasn't one of them. Barry Briggs and Ivan Mauger were the architects of that venture and they had met stadium officials to sort out the basis of a deal before asking me to join them as a partner.

I said yes immediately because I felt it was a surefire winner but before we could set out selling the idea of racing on glazed concrete to the public, and trying to move 7,500 tickets, we had to sell it to Speedway Control Board boss Dick Bracher. He had to give his permission first and we knew he was a stickler for everything being right and proper. But even he surprised us when he walked out into the middle of the arena to do what was, to all intents and purposes, a track inspection.

One of the first things he did, in true speedway fashion, was to dig his heel into the surface and, bearing in mind it was a concrete, he didn't get very far at all. I couldn't believe it, especially when he said it was a bit hard. Anyway, he gave us clearance, subject to him seeing some bikes going round and we were in business after satisfying Wembley's doubts over noise and oil spillage.

Every one of the five meetings between 1979 and 1983 was sponsored by Lada Cars and every one was filmed for transmission on ITV's World Of Sport programme. The first one was the biggest gamble, not from an attendance point of view because I knew it would be a sell-out. My worry was whether or not the idea would work on a concrete track that was only 100 yards long with nothing to provide the grip needed by the bikes to hold them up. The fans were certainly prepared to give it a chance because I took 400 tickets to a meeting when my Hull team were riding at Hackney and sold the lot.

I decided that myself, Barry and the then Speedway Star editor, Philip Rising, who had been seconded to the organising team, should wear evening dress at the meeting with Ivan being excused because he was riding in it. They did it in boxing and we really looked the part but if we thought we'd cracked it by booking the stadium and riders before putting on smart suits, we had another think coming.

Firstly, we had a problem amongst ourselves. Ivan wanted paying for his contribution as a rider, as well as taking his share of the profit. Briggo and I didn't feel that was right and said we would drop him from the line-up if that was what he wanted. We told him he could help us promote the show on the day, rather than ride in it, and he came round to our way of thinking. He rode for nothing and that was probably a first for Ivan.

When you hire Wembley Stadium, you do it for a 24-hour period which means you can move in at midnight and you have to be out by midnight. If not, you incur horrendous penalties. We always followed a gymnastics championship or five-a-side soccer and we always had to work through the night to get everything ready in time for the meeting.

We had toyed with the idea of putting down a loose, dirt surface to give the riders a bit of grip but decided against it for two reasons. One was the time factor and the danger of facing those penalties while we cleaned up afterwards. The other was we felt the novelty of indoor speedway was that the paying public could sit in comfort without any threat from the weather or of being sprayed with dirt. We thought that dressing the officials in dinner suits would help to prove the point and give the proceedings a good image.

One of the biggest jobs was to do all the electrical work and that was so specialised for a speedway meeting we had an agreement with the stadium officials to bring in our man. The unions had a closed shop at Wembley and, while they agreed to let us bring in our own electrician, I soon found out just how closed that shop was. My son, Lyndon, who was six or seven at the time, had come with me. Like most kids, he wanted to help so, to keep him happy, I gave him a brush and told him to sweep the middle of track. Believe it or not, he caused a strike. The entire Wembley staff downed tools and walked out because he was deemed to be scab labour. It cost us about an hour before they came back and got on with the job again after I'd confiscated his brush. I sent him off to count tickets and that was permissible!

There was another problem, which was entirely personal and of little consequence in the greater scheme of things. Phil Rising had what seemed the good idea at the time of introducing walkie talkie sets so we could stay in close contact with each other without having to wander round Wembley searching for whoever we needed to talk to. I soon came to hate them and it wasn't long before I turned mine off and even twisted the antenna to make it less inclined to work. It seemed to be going off all the time and I was tempted to put a notice round my neck saying: 'My name isn't Ian Thomas.' At one point, Phil, Barry and Ivan were standing together and tried to ring me. I ducked down just a few feet away and talked back to them without the walkie talkie. They never twigged.

We had booked World class riders for the meeting but one of the problems beyond our control was that they couldn't come into Wembley to practise until the day of the meeting and, even before that, we had to work in a frenzy to erect the safety fence, starting gate, the pits and lights. And, when the riders did get out there, it was carnage. Everyone had problems with the concrete surface and were falling off left, right and centre. They were having great difficulty staying on, never mind racing, but I left them to practise while I went back to the hotel to put on my dinner suit.

It will be all right on the night, I thought. I'd just had a shower when the phone rang. It was Briggo and he sounded desperate. He told me that the practice carnage had got even worse after I'd left and the riders had decided they couldn't or wouldn't race. They were loading up their bikes to go home just as we were preparing to admit 7,500 people. Briggo asked what should we do and I said: 'Lock 'em in.' There is a big yard behind the arena which is used for bringing in all the gear needed at pop shows and concerts. That's where the pits were situated and there was a big gate at the back. Barry had it locked and I returned to the stadium about 20 minutes later, having given the situation time to cool down.

I had a meeting with Barry, Ivan and Phil in our temporary office and said the one thing that would persuade them to ride would be extra money. So we called in the riders, put some more cash on the table and agreed to pay for any damage to their machinery. They all got a rise – except Ivan of course! So the show was back on the road but we had gone very close to a disaster.

Ironically, the only man who wasn't getting paid won the meeting but there was no suggestion of it being fixed in favour of one of the promoters. Anyone could see Ivan had mastered the concrete surface better than anyone else. The fans either loved it or hated it but it was spectacular and different and that probably explains why it ran for five years. Despite the crashes, especially in the early days, we had only one real injury in those five years and that was when Anders Michanek broke an ankle.

Another much smaller disaster happened on the night which reflected on me – I didn't have enough programmes printed. In those days you could reckon on 70 per cent of the crowd buying a programme. The figure is not so high these days but I estimated we'd sell around 5,250. Even so, I decided on a print run of 8,000. Briggo went nuts, saying we were wasting money. But I said some fans would buy more than one because it was a special occasion and, boy, was I right. We sold out, which meant lost profit.

The same happened last season at Belle Vue when we produced a special programme for the Elite League Play-off final against Coventry. Fans were buying them ten at a time, especially those from Coventry who were getting them for their mates, and we'd sold out a long time before the start. More lost profit and I understand they have been fetching good money on e-bay.

The first Wembley indoor was, at the end of the day, a success but there was a sting in the tail that annoyed me intensely. The touts had got wind of the fact that the tickets were selling well and had moved in to buy their own supply. They were charging treble the price on the black market outside the stadium. If I'd known that was going to happen, I would have held a couple of hundred back and had my late father, George, out there selling them rather than having the touts making money out of our hard work.

There were a lot of falls but there was some cracking racing and the atmosphere in a packed arena was amazing. We had put on other great attractions and just the fact it was Wembley made it special. We also had discos, Malcolm Simmons came out roller-skating, Chris Morton did a tightrope walk after first performing it at Belle Vue circus and we also had a top American stunt rider called Doug Democos. That got me another rollicking from Briggo when he heard I'd booked him. He was a big-time attraction in the States who cost thousands of dollars a show even then. That's why Barry wasn't happy – until I told him he was appearing for nothing.

A guy came up to me at practice and said he managed Democos. I asked who the hell he was and he told me. He was working in Bristol and I said he could stay there because we'd spent the budget. He said he didn't want any money because it would enable him to put Wembley on his CV. I asked if he would do an audition and there was virtually nowhere in the arena where he didn't take that bike. He was fantastic and, being the generous kind of chap I am, I kindly agreed to let him appear for nothing. I told Briggo I had done my best but couldn't get him any cheaper. The first event was extremely profitable, despite having to give the riders that rise.

My day job, of course, was running Hull speedway and, prior to one of the later indoor meetings, we had a match at Reading following talks with the Wembley management to sort out some details. I was due to team manage Hull, as usual, but got stuck in heavy traffic on the M4 and it was the only time in my life that I was late for a match. Ivan, who was riding for me at the time, had also been at Wembley. He was driving a Mercedes and I had a Rolls Royce at the time. We did 100 miles an hour down the hard shoulder but it was still heat four when we arrived. Phil Rising had also gone to Reading and he managed the team until we arrived.

The first Wembley show was the only one that sold out although the second one came close. The third had a fair drop, four was a bit down on that and the last one attracted 3,500 people. We calculated that if we suffered the same percentage reduction again then a sixth show would be borderline and could lose money so we called it a day. I learned a lot from the Wembley experience and one lesson I absorbed from the box office, who have booked all the world's great acts, is how to 'dress a house.' Basically, that means making an auditorium look full when it isn't. There's nothing worse than huge gaps in the audience, especially when you are on TV and it looks as if there is nobody there.

The arena holds 7,500 but the Wembley people can make it look fairly full with 4,500 inside and that is important when it comes to generating atmosphere. It's easy enough to do because they will sell four seats in a row and miss two, then sell three more and miss another. The result is amazing and it is a system that is used by all arenas.

We had a lot of fun over the five years, amidst the problems. In 1982 the Wembley security people called me to say they were ejecting a bloke who said his name was Custard because he was trying to con his way in without paying. He was, in fact, half of an interval attraction of two clowns called Rhubarb and Custard. You couldn't make it up, could you?

My other abiding memory of the Wembley days was when we made a pre-meeting visit to look at the facilities. There was a tennis tournament on at the time and I poked my head into a dressing room to check it out. Jimmy Connors was in there. He looked up at me and said 'XXXX off.' They are the only words he has ever spoken to me.

Where Telford all began – Phil Collins (grounded) and Jan Andersson take a spin
on ice for a party of journalists on a magical mystery tour

16 – Telford: a long-running saga

I ADMITTED in the previous chapter that I couldn't take the credit for dreaming up the idea of running speedway on concrete at the Wembley Arena and the same applies to the Telford ice spectacular. My business partner, Graham Drury, is responsible for this one and as it was the 21st anniversary of the show in 2006 we must be doing something right.

Graham was riding for me at Hull when the concept struck him and he had been testing spikes in tyres at one or two rinks before he satisfied Wrekin Council, the owners of Telford, that it was possible to stage speedway racing on ice. They had been very concerned it would ruin the rink.

Graham was still riding at that time and had no experience of promoting. He rang me to say he'd got an idea and would I like to discuss it with him over a game of golf. We did just that at the Hawksworth Club where I once had a hole in one when playing with Barry Briggs. Graham outlined his plan to stage a two-day show using junior riders so, if it didn't work, there wouldn't be too much of a financial loss.

I told him that I thought the scheme was dynamite but I didn't like the two-day idea and I didn't think it was best to use juniors. Broadly, we had a good plan that needed a lot of polishing. I agreed we had the two meetings but proposed to run them both in one day as people might pay to watch two shows in a day, which they do, but wouldn't travel twice in two days. Also, we would only have one rental to pay and it would save riders' expenses if they didn't have to come for two days. I also wanted to use some of the World's top riders instead of banking on juniors. We agreed, did a deal and we are still going strong.

Our first move after deciding the idea was a runner was to organise a big publicity launch so we called in Richard Bott, my Press Officer at Hull, to help us sort it out. Richard was convinced it wouldn't work but we whetted the Press appetite by inviting them to a hotel near the M6 in Birmingham with the promise of a good story. That started the alarm bells ringing amongst Midland promoters as the media speculated that a new track was opening and two even turned up at the hotel to find out what was happening.

We loaded the Press gang onto a coach for a mystery tour and

whisked them away to Telford and let the story unfurl. Riders Jan
Andersson and Phil Collins were waiting at the rink to give a
demonstration. They roared out from behind a curtain with ice
flying. It was dramatic and the media lads were hooked. We had
coverage in all the nationals and TV so, within a day, we had achieved
a massive impact and virtually everyone in speedway knew about the
new venture.

I have to confess that I wasn't convinced it would work but it did.
Dick Bott says that he still wasn't convinced when we staged the first
meeting and reckons he stood by the pit exit ready to do a runner if
necessary. But the first meeting was a sell-out, the fans loved it and
the stadium hasn't been far from full ever since. We have brought in
riders from all over the world and tried something different every
year, based on the same format, so people would keep coming. We
used all kinds of publicity ideas including sending invitations to the
Royal Family and Prime Minister one year and getting Alun Rossiter
to ride round the rink stark naked. That stunt got his picture in the
Daily Sport, amongst others.

The best extra attraction we ever had was when we booked the real
World Ice champion, Swede Erik Stenlund, on his real ice racing bike.
We put him on during the interval of the afternoon show and he was
sensational, even though he nearly ruined the ice with the power and
traction he was able to produce. The only snag was that he made our
boys, on their adapted bikes, look silly. I had a quiet word with
Graham before the evening show and made the sensible decision to
switch the timetable and put him on last so the fans couldn't compare
the relative speeds to the same extent. Wayne Dobson, the illusionist,
was another attraction who went down a storm.

We've had very few injuries over the years, despite the fears of the
riders that they could get cut up by the spikes in the back tyres. The
most spectacular crash we ever had was suffered by Midland boy Neil
Evitts, even though he is unlikely to agree. We have a gap in the safety
fence by the starting gate and, beyond that gap, is a door which we
leave open so the fumes can escape. Neil lost control of his bike and
not only did he go through the gap in the fence, he went through the
door as well and went down four steps to finish up outside the
stadium – complete with his bike. Fortunately, he was only badly
shaken and the damage could have been much worse.

Jan Andersson, Andy Campbell and Hans Nielsen were the top
dogs in those early days but Jan and Hans were World class riders
anyway. More recently Denmark's team manager, Jan Staechmann,

has been one of the most consistent riders but we've had a lot of superstars there over the years like Tomasz Gollob and Nicki Pedersen. We have never made the mistake of trying to sell Telford as conventional speedway but it is competitive and the riders have got harder and harder as time as moved on. Nielsen commented in his era that he thought it was becoming too hard. But, basically, it is a fun, entertaining event and a great social get-together just before the season opens in March.

One of my regrets is that my Workington captain and local legend Carl Stonehewer hates the ice stuff. It would be great business for us to use him at Telford because he would attract fans down from Cumbria. He did it one year and couldn't get round as he would have liked but I decided he would be an attraction even if he wasn't riding. So we set him the challenge of doing as many different jobs as he could during the one day of the show. That got us good pre-publicity and the idea was a rip-roaring success on the day because he kept popping up, sometimes in the most unexpected places such as when he was the ladies toilet attendant! He filled about 20 roles on the day which included being the announcer, a programme seller, a car park attendant and a barman. It was funny and it gave the day something extra which was very pleasing for me because it was a daft idea that worked. Mike Patrick, the Speedway Star's chief photographer, followed Carl around and got some great pictures so we cashed in as well with some superb extra publicity afterwards.

The joy of running at Telford is that we are not at the mercy of the weather, even in February. We can't get rained off and the only real threat to the show is a power cut because we need electricity to maintain the correct temperature for the ice. The rink manager did come up to Graham and myself a few years ago to say there were problems because the ice was melting. That sent a shiver down our backs! She said we would get through the first show but, while it wasn't a power cut, something had gone wrong with the machinery under the ice and it wouldn't last out for the evening performance if it couldn't be fixed. We had to find a specialist on a Sunday afternoon to come out to look at the pipes and, thankfully, he mended it. Even so, the ice had gone soft and it took a long time to freeze up again with the result that the first show was naff.

I believe in publicity, as you will have gathered, but we were close to attracting some we didn't want when we had Skol Bandits as our sponsor. It was a kind of chewing tobacco and the researchers for Esther Rantzen's That's Life consumer programme came on during

the run-up to the meeting. It was in our contract that we couldn't
have cigarette manufacturers as a sponsor because we were racing on
council property and they asked some awkward questions. We had
cleared it as being okay to use the sponsorship but That's Life
wouldn't let go and tried very hard to get us on the programme to
discuss the situation. We avoided that interview like the plague,
probably the only time I've ducked a TV spot.

The success of Telford led to us promoting a Christmas event at
Milton Keynes that was a good show which just about covered itself.
We had interest from several ice rinks and sold the show to the
owners of Murrayfield in Edinburgh and Dundonald in Northern
Ireland. Then we went to Bordeaux, in France, and numerous rinks
in Germany. I have a special memory of Bordeaux because we booked
a French rider, who had better remain unidentified for legal reasons,
to attract the local fans. The riders went out by van and we took Paul
Ackroyd to referee the meeting. He had a ride to Bordeaux with the
French lad and looked distinctly shaken when he arrived. I asked him
if there was a problem. He told me that every time they had stopped
for petrol, his driver had jumped straight back into the van and done
a runner without paying. Paul was sitting there fearing the worst for
his ACU licence. I told him to calm down and took him out into
Bordeaux old town where we had a couple of bottles of wine – that I
paid for!

We also went to Geneva and Zurich in Switzerland and have been
approached to take a show to a rink in Budapest, Hungary so that
would be another first. Apart from Europe, we have even staged
racing on an ice rink in the middle of a desert in the United Arab
Emirates at Al Ain, which is 70 miles from Dubai. That started
through me phoning a contact in a theme park there because I had
noticed there was a rink when I had been out to work on a magic
show. We were invited to negotiate a deal to take a troupe of riders and
I remember there was a British wrestling show out there at the same
time. One of them was called The Little Prince from Pakistan who, I
discovered, had a garage in Harehills, Leeds, not far from my home.
Another was a guy calling himself Colonel Bogey who wouldn't talk
to anyone. There is usually a good guy and a bad guy in wrestling
bouts but the thing that amazed me about these boys was that, socially,
the goodies stuck with the goodies and the baddies stayed the baddies.

We signed a contract to take the ice show out a year later and, on the
way back, we stayed over in Dubai because I knew the Hyatt Regency
hotel had an ice rink in the foyer. We met the manager, an American,

who showed us round but it was clear the rink wasn't big enough for our purposes. He asked us if we could ride bikes on the ice to music. I said it was no problem, apart from the fact that no-one would be able to hear the music for the noise of the bikes.

When we returned to Al Ain for the big festival, which celebrated the end of Ramadan, the riders we took were Keith White, Richard Hellsen, Alun Rossiter and Simon Cross. We were there for nearly three weeks, doing one show a day, and we had a great time.

I got very friendly with the Pakistani vet who looked after the ruler's racing camels which can be worth millions. Cross still had some stitches in his head from a crash in the speedway season and wanted them taking out. He asked if the insurance for the trip would cover the cost but it didn't apply to injuries that had occurred before the trip. So I had a word with the camel specialist and asked him if he would remove the stitches which he did. Crossy wasn't too impressed at the time but it was cheap. He was more impressed when he joined me for a game of golf at the Emirates Club, in Dubai which was something else. Jasper Carrott was behind us.

We were pulling capacity crowds in a 4,000 arena for our shows. I doubled up as the commentator and Rossiter was adding to the drama by doing his dying swan act when he came off. It turned into a crying wolf act when he took a real purler in a corner halfway through a show. He stayed down with the bike on top of him but I thought he was at it again and took no notice until I realised the ice was turning red. Blood red.

We got him to hospital where Graham Drury and myself went to see him as soon as the show was finished. We were greeted by an Egyptian doctor who said the injury was bad and that they would have to amputate his leg. That really stopped us in our tracks. We knew the spikes on the back wheel had dug in to Rosco's leg but we hadn't realised it was as bad as this. The doctor took us to see the X-rays and thank God he did. He put them up on a screen for us to examine. I looked carefully and said: 'My rider has injured the other leg, not that one.' The X-rays were for a 70-year-old Indian woman. I'm not saying they would have removed Rosco's leg without further checks but it was still a close enough call.

The next job was to visit him on the ward and tell him the good news. Notices over there are printed in Arabic and English and we saw a sign saying Prisoners' Ward. I went in for a look. It held five or six beds but there was one person in there, an old guy who was 75 if he was a day. He was shackled by his hands and legs to his bed. I wished him all the best and went to find Rosco who was kicking up a row as usual about his injury. Graham and I told him he'd have to stay in overnight at least for a course of injections and warned him he would have to grit his teeth because the needles might be on the blunt side. He was still shouting and moaning so Graham and I, noticing there were no nurses about, wheeled his bed into the Prisoners' Ward and left him there. He was doing his nut but at least the old guy had some company!

One of the performers at the festival was a half Cherokee Indian from Liverpool. He did a knife throwing act but also said he was a hypnotist. Rosco was soon out of hospital so we arranged for him and Crossy to be hypnotised at the hotel and a lot of people came along to watch. To be frank, I think hypnosis is a load of rubbish but this was hilarious and people were doubled up with laughter when the pair of them were talking to each other in moon language. It was absolute gibberish.

Carl Stonehewer, Wayne Broadhurst, Martin Dixon and Kevin Little went on the second trip and to have Stoney in the Middle East, with all their strict rules, was something else. I didn't know much about him when we went but I certainly did by the time we returned. We used Honda 125 bikes to cut down on the cost of air-freight and they were very good. I also took an illusionist called Jimmy Carlo, who was 30 stone, with his eight stone assistant Crystal, who was also his wife. Stoney called him Jimmy Five Bellies.

We went out in the desert one day for some four-wheel driving in the dunes and a camel ride. We had trouble finding a camel that could lift Jimmy but, finally, we took off with them tied together in a line. I was at the back and Stoney, the sod, cut mine loose, gave it a whack and I took off at speed. Not only was it terrifying to be on the back of a runaway camel, it took them an hour to find me by which time I wasn't really seeing the joke. I didn't know where I was going and, even worse, I kept thinking that these animals can keep running for days. I owed Stoney for that big style and, later in the trip, all his clothes went missing for four days.

We were always pulling stunts on each other. When we went to Geneva, Hans Nielsen, an expert skier, said he was going on the slopes with his wife, Suzanne. Bernie Collier, from Belle Vue, and Geoff Powell, from Workington said they fancied a go. I told them the black run was the one for novices and they fell for it. It took them six hours to get down. I also told Geoff, better known as Leggy, that they had snowball throwing competitions in Geneva. He said he fancied a go but he changed his mind when I told him it cost 30p a snowball but when I told him we could go to see the Swiss Navy he seemed to fancy that!

Not so funny for one of the lads, who had better remain anonymous, was an episode on one of two trips to Barcelona. We were part of a show which included a brilliant pick-pocket act but we met a real one. We were told of a red light area close to the football stadium so the riders piled in a van with Graham Drury driving and me in the passenger seat to take a look. We stopped and one of the riders made the mistake of opening a door for a closer look. One of the ladies of the night moved in, grabbed him in the most painful place you can imagine and lifted his wallet while he was fighting her off. She didn't get much, though. He was a tight sod at the best of times.

We have a saying that riders don't earn much on a Thomas-Drury trip but they have a bloody good time. I think that is true.

The most incredible daredevil of them ALL!

SAY HELLO AT THE EASTER SHOW

HENRI La Mothe

the big flop

His name is Henri LaMothe, and he is a genial little gentleman of 70 years, a man with a strong face and a husky chest, who often wears a beret and a dapper thin gray moustache and a man who makes a living in a way different from anyone else in the world.

Visitors to the San Antonio World's Fair, who've seen his splashy show, think he's the greatest, even though he claims to be the biggest flop in show business.

Henri, who weighs approximately 150 pounds soaking wet, climbed to the top of a 40 foot tower at Hemisfair for six weeks, swan diving into space and making a belly-busting dive into a small pool of water only 17 inches deep . . . coming up smiling, which you have to admit takes a lot of guts, and performing the trick twice a day.

He developed the act, he says, by jumping off bridges and out of hotel windows into concrete wading pools.

"I have never missed", he says, convincingly, as if you might not believe him, "and I've been at it almost 20 years. No, I don't have any immediate plans for quitting because I haven't grown tired of what I'm doing. It's always a challenge. I'm allowed one mistake and I haven't made it yet. I don't expect to, either. If I miss the pool, you see, the sponsors don't pay me".

LaMothe, who stands just 5-7, remembers making his first belly whopper at the age of four. And ever since, water has had a fascination for him. The smell of it excites him. He took his first high dive when he was 12, leaping from 55 feet high into seven feet of water. That little adventure cost him his only scar to date . . . a cut over his eye.

He started in show biz as a clown in water shows —a job that involved a large number of crash landings on the water. After a few of these, he decided he didn't need all that water. The secret, he points out, is not to hit the water flat.

"You are going about 35 miles an hour when you hit, see, and you would be ripped open if you hit flat. I hit the water stomach first, with my shoulders and hips arched back. That's why nobody else can do the dive. They can't stomach it".

Landing in this position, he notes, his stomach cleaves the water and reduces the force of impact. Seventeen inches of water is enough, even though he confessed he's gotten by with just 15½ inches in practice. That's cutting it too thin, he agreed.

"Sometimes I feel my stomach touch the bottom of the pool, but it is always after the force of the dive is gone. Then I just stand up and see how many spectators got wet in the splash. One time, I doused a mayor and two councilmen. The only problem I have is with outdoor performances, when the wind can ruin my timing.

"You might say I'm ill when a wind blows", he mused.

LaMothe is a native of Chicago who now makes his home in New York City.

17 – Man in the Iron Mask: 1750

FORMER rider Graham Drury has been involved with me in a variety of business ventures over the years with the Telford Indoor Ice show the best known and most successful.

Less known are the specialty acts we used to do, all in the name of entertaining the public and making a few quid at country fairs, agricultural shows and ice rinks. If you have ever seen acts called the Man In The Iron Mask or Catching A Bullet In Your Teeth it was us.

The iron mask act involved being blindfolded and hooded before driving a car or riding a bike round human obstacles in an arena or an ice rink. We would ask a member of the public to inspect the mask and hood that we used to ensure that it was impossible to see through them and then drive around without hitting anyone.

I remember one show at Cardiff when we were booked to appear at an ice variety show that was being shown live on TV. Other acts included singers Mel and Kim, the British bobsleigh team and a pop group called Living In A Box. Graham and I had to go to Cardiff the day before to rehearse and we were made to hang around for hours for our turn. It went fine and we arrived at the rink the next morning, prepared the bike and asked the way to our dressing room. The producer pointed to a door, we went in and couldn't believe our eyes. We were sharing with six penguins – and they were nasty little sods as well.

We used the presenters and TV staff to ride round. It went well but, looking back, perhaps we should have roped in those pesky penguins!

We also did the iron mask show live at the Dundonald rink, on the outskirts of Belfast. It was for Children In Need and Graham and myself had flown over with former Belle Vue and Newcastle rider, Bernie Collier, and a mate employed to bring the bike over on the ferry. We used one of Bernie's machines because they were always reliable and ran well. Little did we know. The rehearsal went well and, come show time, Graham and I did a live interview before taking a five-minute break while the human obstacles were put in place for Graham to ride round. Great. Bernie, who was stationed outside so the noise of the bike starting wouldn't be heard on TV, was told he would be given a minute's warning to get his machine running. So we came back, I went into my patter, Bernie was told a minute – and the reliable bike wouldn't start! Panic stations. I saw a go-kart at the side of the rink, which had been used for another act, so I told Graham to jump into that instead. The viewers who had seen him sitting on a bike in the build-up to the act, complete with a back wheel full of ferocious looking spikes, then watched him perform in a go-kart. The producer was none too pleased to say the least.

We had done a TV show to publicise the event and were heading for the studio in a taxi from our hotel when I told Bernie and his mate that we were approaching the most famous prison in Ireland where they detained all the major criminals. I said they did tours three times a day and it was only £2.50 to go round. I said I'd been and it was good. Bernie hadn't sussed it was a wind-up but he didn't fancy it. His mate, however, did want to go so we stopped the taxi and I pointed out a guy with a machine gun. I said: 'He's the one who takes the money.' Off he went, starting to get his cash out until the soldier invited him to go away – NOW. It's the best wind-up I've ever pulled.

We once appeared on a two-day show at Teesside, second on the bill behind Mickey and Minnie Mouse with the White Helmets third. If we did the iron mask act on a bike Graham would do it and, if we were using a car, I would do it. It was my turn to drive and the performance was outdoors at Middlesbrough. It's difficult to tell this story without giving too much away but, just before we were due to go out, it started to rain. We'd had the mask and hood checked to prove I couldn't see out and the volunteer had also examined the car for electronic devices. I even had a member of the public sitting next to me but it's fair to say that it is an illusion and there is a way of achieving a degree of visibility which remains a secret. Graham was preparing to do the patter when a few drops began to fall. I shouted: 'It's starting to rain.' He said: 'What's the problem with that?' I replied: 'We'll look a couple of dickheads if I go out there supposedly unable to see anything but with the windscreen wipers on!' Luckily, it was a passing cloud and the shower soon moved away.

The bullet catching act earned us the nickname of the Bullet Brothers from Press man Richard Bott and we hated doing it because, over a period of time, eight people had been killed performing it. That doesn't strike me as a bad reason for doing something else with your time. We had a trestle stand, rather like an artist's easel, which had a plate standing in the middle. The gun was handed to a member of the audience who fired at the plate which smashed to pieces to prove the ammunition was live.

The spectator then put a mark on another bullet, so it could be identified at the end of the act. It was loaded into the gun which was then handed to me. Dramatic stuff. Graham would do a couple of circuits of the arena on his motor cycle and then head straight for me in the centre. I would fire the gun at him, he would catch the bullet in his teeth and fall off the bike. That was the easy bit for Graham but it always had a good effect on the crowd.

The spectator would take a plate up to Graham, he would spit the bullet onto it and then our helper would examine it before confirming that his mark was there. It was a great illusion and people loved it because Graham hadn't been within 50 yards of me or the volunteer at any time.

Part of my job as the patter merchant was to find the spectator who would mark the bullet and, without being too rude, I would try to pick someone who looked a sandwich short of a picnic. We got a booking to do both acts at the two-day Bury Show, in Lancashire, and we'd performed the Iron Mask without a hitch. Then it was time to bite the bullet again and I asked a bloke to come out to help.

I gave him the gun and bullets to examine so he could confirm they were real and asked him to confirm they were real. It was a good job that I always kept the microphone switched off at this time. He looked at me and asked: 'Are you taking the mickey?' There was a feeling of panic as I replied: 'What do you mean, sir.' He said: 'I'm a munitions expert in the Army.' I'd picked the wrong gentleman and he certainly was a full picnic. He had got me by the proverbials. I said: 'Do us a favour, go along with it and I'll buy you a couple of pints afterwards.' He did and I duly met up with him again in the beer tent.

We once went on a show called Sky Star Search in London with the bullet act. I don't know why we did it because I wasn't that keen but we finished up being judged by a panel that included Nicky Campbell, who I don't like, Wendy Richard and Keith Chegwin, who was the chairman. We had to wait in a room until we were called for rehearsal and a comedian who went down before us was nearly crying when he came back. That put the wind up us but we asked what had happened. He said he'd told six jokes and they'd said none of them were suitable for a family audience. We suggested the easy way out was to tell six more. He said: 'I don't know any more.'

He had just written in asking if he could appear and they had put him on. I told him to go out and tell those six jokes again and leave the problem of their suitability to the TV people. We wore suits for our act that made us look like Italian waiters, according to Nicky Campbell, but we got through it okay, even though it was clear the panel weren't very complimentary. At the end of the show, all the acts had to line up on stage and wave and the one that came last was awarded a model pig. What garbage. Five or six acts had taken part and we stood there in dread of getting the pig because we would never live it down. But it went to the six-joke comedian. Perhaps it should have been the sick-joke comedian. What a laugh!

We once took the bullet act on Opportunity Knocks and in the rehearsal I shot the plate that flew into a million pieces. The producer went white and pulled the plug on the rest of our act. He said: 'You didn't tell me you were going to make a mess. We're running late and we've got some dancers coming on next with the stage covered in bits of plate.'

You might say what a way to make a living but we had some great years doing it and the fees were good. We performed at most of the ice rinks in the United Kingdom, where people had never seen anything like our acts before, and also at venues right across Europe, including the magnificent Ahoy Stadium in Rotterdam.

18 – Starr turns in speedway

I'M one of the few promoters to use showbusiness personalities and other novelty attractions to bring people through the turnstiles. I have mentioned elsewhere in the book success of having comedians Ken Dodd at Workington and Freddie Starr at Hull. They proved massively successful but they are only a tiny proportion of the people and acts I have booked.

People often ask me why I spend money on extra entertainment and the answer, quite simply, is that I'm a businessman and I wouldn't do it if I didn't think it would generate income. Apart from being a promoter, I like to think I'm a showman as well. After all I work as a magician and run my own Ian Thomas Organisation which is an entertainment agency that takes bookings from all over the world.

I have a definite policy over booking attractions and it may come as a surprise because the obvious time to do it would seem to be when you have a poor team coming, or local holidays, and want to boost the gate. That's what promoters like Reg Fearman used to do in the days when bringing in the stars and other acts was more prevalent.

But I think that is wrong from a commercial point of view. What is the point of drawing in extra people to watch what you think is going to be a poor match? It may pay a dividend on the night but are the public going to come back if they have seen a bad night's racing? The answer to that is no, they are not.

I book attractions when I think I have got a good fixture. You can never be sure of that in speedway because even a match between the top two teams can be disappointing. But if you attract new people and put on a cracking match then, hopefully, they'll come back for more and you have a chance of turning them into speedway fans.

I accept that not all regular fans like the attractions and they include Speedway Star editor Richard Clark with whom I have had some fierce discussions on the topic. Some supporters only want to come along to see the racing and I respect that, but I have a business to run and it is my job to get people through the gate.

But whenever I put on an attraction, I never increase the admission price. That way, fans cannot complain that they have been made to pay extra for something they don't want. If they don't want to see it for free, they can go for a beer. The promotion absorbs the cost and, obviously, I wouldn't do it if I didn't think that investment was profitable.

Another reason I make these bookings is the potential for extra column inches in the newspapers as well as coverage on local TV, radio and other media outlets. You can't buy that kind of space because editorial cover has greater impact than paid-for adverts, so the extra publicity you are given is another source of payback. It all adds up.

Having said that, I didn't do it at Belle Vue in my first season but the reason for that was that I had a cracking attraction for the first night with the presence of the club's World Champions.

An attraction will work even better if you can involve a rider in it. An example of that, which I remember well, was in the 1970s when I booked the late Colin Crompton, famous for the Wheeltappers and Shunters Social Club, at Newcastle. He did ten minutes on the centre green at the interval, presented the trophies at the end and then he witnessed Tom Owen signing his new contract for the following season. That picture went all over the place and the space it earned us more than paid his fee without considering the extra people he brought in and the entertainment he provided.

I have a friend called Philip Hitchcock, a top illusionist with whom I work a great deal, and I asked him if he could involve a rider with his act on the centre green. Some wouldn't do it, but he agreed. He did an illusion at Workington with an open structure shaped like a tent. Everyone could see through it but then there was a big bang and the curtains dropped. Normally his assistant would walk out but he agreed to a switch and, when the curtains fell, our captain Carl Stonehewer was standing there. He'd had to come up to Derwent Park early in the day for a rehearsal but it went off brilliantly and the crowd went crackers. So did Kenny Fearon, our start marshal who was only a few feet away from where it happened. We'd only just had the parade and he said: 'Where the hell did he come from? He's only just gone back into the pits with the rest of the riders on a truck."

I was in the Dragonara Hotel in Leeds one night with Brian Larner and we saw Max Bygraves in the bar. We went up and asked him if he wanted to earn extra pounds presenting trophies and telling a few gags at Hull speedway the next night. We did a deal, he came along and he was a very nice man.

I also booked Hughie Green, star of the Opportunity Knocks and Double Your Money programmes, to appear when I was promoting at Barrow. I have to be honest and say that I was never a fan but he was a big star. I wasn't happy with the answer when he arrived and I asked what he was going to do. He said he'd brought five sets of corsets with him and he wanted five riders to go out at the interval to see who could put them on the fastest. He said the winner would get a prize and I thought to myself: 'That sounds naff.' It showed how much I knew because he brought the house down but, probably, the secret of his success that night was that he was wise enough to involve the riders. It was funny, though.

Hughie and I were staying in the same hotel in Barrow that night and we sat up late talking and having quite a few drinks. It was then that I said I wasn't keen on watching him on TV. He didn't take offence but said: 'In that case you are clever. Even though you didn't like me yourself, you still booked me because you knew the public did.' He was right because he pulled me a crowd.

The spin-off from that was that I got Joe Owen on his Double Your Money quiz programme that was a massive game show at the time. It gave us huge, extra publicity. Hughie liked the idea of having a young man who lived dangerously on his show and it was taped at Tyne Tees studios. They always gave a contestant an easy question to get going and, bearing in mind Joe came from farming stock, he was asked what sheep dip was used for. I couldn't believe it but he didn't know and failed to get any further than question one. But we still got good mileage out of it.

I used an Irish guy called Blondini a few times. He used to blow himself up in a coffin and, since he died, I've booked his son at Workington. Blondini was a real character and, like other people I'd used up there, I arranged for him to do an interview on Border TV's Look Around show to get some extra publicity before coming to the track from the studios in Carlisle. They had a young presenter doing his first live show and, halfway through the interview, Blondini put his hand in his pocket and pulled out a real 150 watt bulb. He started to eat it. It threw the presenter and he said: 'What are you doing?' Blondini kept munching away and replied in his broad Irish accent: 'Having my tea.' There was no answer to that and it finished the youngster totally. He didn't even ask him if it was a light meal!

Another act I booked on a regular basis was Don Lindberg who had a six-foot tank of water and a 70-foot tower. He would pour petrol on top of the water and climb the tower. His assistant would ignite the water and he would set fire to himself before diving into the tank and extinguishing the flames. He told me the secret was to turn as he hit the water or he would have gone through the bottom of the tank. It was an amazing act and I thought there was no justice that a guy who earned his living in such a dangerous way should die of cancer.

One of the most unusual high diving acts was an American gentleman called Henry LeMoth, who was still performing at the age of 71. The legendary Evel Knievel came over in the 1970s for a UK tour which opened at Wembley. It never got any further because Knievel nearly killed himself and all the supporting acts, of which Henry was one, suddenly became available for bookings because the tour was scrapped. I used him at three of the four tracks I was running at the time. He used to belly flop from a 40-foot tower into a foot of water and was one of the best attractions I ever booked.

Charlie Williams was a top comedian when I used to book him and we agreed to have an early round of golf at Hawksworth, near Leeds, before going up to Workington. I was a relatively new member there and it was a bit posh. There was a ladies competition arranged but I got permission to play. He was acting the clown a bit as we went round and the ladies were asking him for his autograph as we passed them. It was fun until the lady captain came up and asked Charlie to sign a golf ball. I nearly died when he asked her: 'Wouldn't you like to play with black balls?' She went red and smiled. When we got back to the clubhouse I spoke to the pro, a smashing guy called Syd Whelden, and asked him if I was in trouble. He said: 'No Ian. They loved it.'

Other acts I've used successfully are the Batmobile, characters from the Planet of the Apes, lookalikes for Prince Charles, James Bond and David Jason as well as the real three-wheel Reliant Robin from Trotters Independent Traders which we got from a museum in Keswick. Lynn Wright, mum of Workington rider James, who is one of speedway's great young talents, made a personal appearance at Workington with her whippet, Didi, after it had won Best in Show at Crufts. I was even the dog's agent for two months.

Actor Bill Maynard came along to a meeting and Pat Phoenix (Elsie Tanner from Coronation Street) opened Ellesmere Port for me and was a very nice lady.

The critics can ask what has all that to do with speedway and the answer is: 'Not a lot.' But, over the years, I can prove that most of them increased attendances, entertained most of the people in the stadium and attracted extra media coverage. There is no doubt that, by and large, they paid for themselves.

19 – Triple wham Bammy

ASK most people to name three of my tracks and they would probably say Workington, Hull and Newcastle. But there are three more, Belle Vue, Barrow and Ellesmere Port where, restless soul that I am, I stayed for only a short time.

The year at Belle Vue, in 1982, was by far the most significant and enjoyable. New promoter Stuart Bamforth brought me in as team manager when Eric Boocock left and we won the British League title by six points from Cradley Heath.

It was a record-breaking fourth title for the Aces but, before I go a step further, I must emphasise that it was with a team that Eric had built. I inherited it and, boy, was I lucky with what he left me.

I received a phone call out of the blue from Bamforth, the stock car promoter and former World stock car champion, who had just bought Hyde Road stadium and the legendary Aces from Trust House Forte. I'd only ever met him a couple of times so I didn't really know him but he laid his cards straight on the table in that call. He said he wanted to employ me for one season only to show him how to be a speedway promoter and a team manager. Eric had left after a difference of opinion with him but, as it was only two years after the pair of us had taken England to the Grand Slam, I felt I was treading on eggs.

Hull, where I had been promoting in the British League, had closed down because of a dispute with our landlords, the Rugby League club. I was still running Newcastle in the Second Division at the time but had space in my diary to do the Belle Vue job. However, I didn't want to be seen as jumping into my mate Eric's shoes so I asked Bammy about what had happened and he just said that it wasn't my problem. Yorkshiremen are known to be blunt but Bammy was a man who never called a spade a shovel and said: 'Are you going to do the job or not?' I said: 'In principle I'll do it.' He replied: 'Xxxx principle. Drive across here and, if we can't do a deal, you can xxxx off home.' You always knew where you stood with Bammy. We met a couple of hours later at Hyde Road, did a deal in five minutes and I was manager of Belle Vue, the most famous speedway team in the world.

Running a team was nothing new to me, of course, but teaching someone else how to do it certainly was. What do you tell someone who wants to learn how to be a team manager? First you need to know the rulebook backwards and then man management and motivation skills come into it. The absolute first thing I'd tell any aspiring team manager to do may sound daft but it's simple: Always have two pens. There's nothing worse than being in a tight situation and having to make decisions under pressure, particularly at the end of a meeting, and your pen runs out. It's so simple yet so important.

Eric left me with a dream team. Chris Morton was top man in my season with an average of more than 10 but just behind him were Kiwi Larry Ross and Peter Collins. The Carr brothers, Louis and Peter, Peter Ravn and my old friend from Hull, Jim McMillan, completed the side and they all did more than 40 matches in a season where I had to make very few team changes. One rider Eric didn't sign for Belle Vue that season was a 16-year-old Yorkshire kid who had been making a big name for himself in grasstrack circles.

Everyone was after him and I was there in the speedway office at Hyde Road when the deal was done. It was, of course, Andy Smith and the wheel had turned full circle in 2005, 23 remarkable years later, when we were together again with the Aces. He didn't do too many meetings in 1982 because he had to wait for his sixteenth birthday before he could start racing but he was still part of the set-up at the start of an amazing career.

Bammy was desperately keen to repeat his stock car success in speedway, even though the cars always remained his first love. He was a quick learner and he was thrilled to win the title. He'd always be looking over my shoulder at meetings and asking me to explain my decisions. It was a pleasure to manage that team, apart from the night when Steve Gresham, a former rider of mine at Hull, kicked me where it hurts.

We were doing well as the season progressed and the championship was boiling down to a battle between Cradley Heath and ourselves. Then we went to Sheffield one Thursday and we got hammered big style. Bammy went nuts. He wasn't one for talking to the Press a great deal but Richard Frost, of the Manchester Evening News, got hold of him in the bar afterwards and obtained the famous quote: 'A team of monkeys on bikes would have done better.'

Talk about motivation. Richard tells me that the lads were upset and some of them had hard words with him about printing it. But it worked. The Aces went through to the end of the season unbeaten and the championship pennant flew at the top of the Hyde Road flagpole. Bammy was learning fast and I was thrilled to be in charge of such a fine set of riders at probably the best track the speedway

THE 2005 Belle Vue Aces celebrate their Knockout Cup victory.

SECRET agent 'James Bond' joins the Workington Comets.

JASON Crump at Belle Vue in 2005

After losing out in the Elite League play-offs in 2005, Ian, Jason Crump and the other Aces were delighted to lift the Knockout Cup.

WORLD Champions in Hull colours.
Above: Barry Briggs. Below: Ivan Mauger.

THE Owen brothers ... Joe (left) and Tom.

WORLD Longtrack Champion Egon Muller who had a short spell at Hull in 1976.

PETER Collins, winner of one of the many top class individual meetings held at Hull's Boulevard Stadium, with Chris Morton (right) and Doug Wyer.

world has ever seen. What a tragedy it was for the sport that Hyde Road is no longer with us.

I think I taught Bammy something about being a team manager and how to manipulate the rules but I didn't help him much to be a promoter because our styles were totally different to say the least. I was very sorry to hear he had passed away a few years ago.

That year is the only time I have won the First Division championship although I went close at Hull in 1979, losing out in the never-to-be-forgotten final match of the season at Coventry who nicked the title by two points. But everyone knows I won it at Belle Vue in 2005!

The team I took over in 1982 wasn't a dead cert to win the title but it was packed with potential. It was a pleasure to watch PC and Mort going round Hyde Road but it was a team effort and I was privileged to manage it. Anyone would have liked to stay on to run that side, especially at that track, but it was essentially a one-year deal because Bammy wanted to do his own thing. There is no question that Hyde Road was a better stadium and better racetrack than what we've got now but Kirkmanshulme Lane provides entertaining racing and is far better than no racing at all.

Wally Mawdsley, the late Bill Carman, who was my announcer at Hull, and myself opened Ellesmere Port in 1972 after buying Rochdale's Second Division licence and also taking on several of their riders. It was the first time speedway had run on Merseyside since Liverpool had closed 12 years earlier. We appointed the well-known and highly respected journalist, the late Frank Maclean, as Press Officer and Colin Tucker came in to build the track which ran round the outside of the town soccer pitch. It was a big, fast racing circuit and Pat Phoenix, who played Elsie Tanner in Coronation Street, was our guest on the opening night, along with the mayor.

The Gunners, as we called the side, had an opening crowd of 1,800 on a nice night and that told me the venture wasn't going to be a runaway success. We had generated a lot of good publicity but it didn't bode well for us that a fair percentage of the fans who came were from the local tracks at Belle Vue, Rochdale and Crewe. We tried hard and didn't have a bad side, which included riders like Paul Tyrer, Graham Drury, Colin Goad and Robbie Gardner, but the only time we got anywhere near that opening night attendance was when we rode the derby match against Crewe.

Maury Littlechild promoted Crewe on behalf of the Allied Presentations consortium and his other business was growing mushrooms. That needs bags and bags of horse manure which he bought from the stables in the Newmarket area and he had a lot of friends in the racing fraternity. Maury once invited me to be his guest at Chester races, complete with a VIP pass for the best enclosures, before our sides met in an evening match at Crewe. I'd always enjoyed going horse racing with my dad so it was great to be there mixing with some of the big names in the racing world. Maury introduced me to top jockey, Willie Carson, and he told us he fancied one of his mounts. We backed it and it won so I had a most enjoyable and profitable day.

Not so enjoyable or profitable was the Ellesmere Port venture and it became increasingly apparent that we were flogging a dead horse rather than a winner. I let it be known discreetly on the grapevine that we may be prepared to listen to offers but I wasn't holding my breath that someone would come forward. But, out of the blue, a fan called Jim Sephton came onto the scene to show an interest. He didn't think we had run it very well and thought he could turn it round. I don't know how many times I've heard that over the years. We sold it to him, having just about broken even, but, sadly, my fears were justified. Sephton's venture didn't work out for him but the Gunners ran for a few more seasons without being a financial success, even in 1985 when they won the Second Division championship under that lovely man, Mervyn Porter, a greengrocer from Bolton. That was the season their star man and my former hero at Newcastle, Joe Owen, had the tragic crash at Birmingham that cost him his career and left him in a wheelchair.

I remember taking Newcastle to race at Ellesmere and a security man flattened one of my boys, Graeme Stapleton, before the meeting. I never discovered what happened but it must have been a real wallop because Graeme was a big lad and he wasn't fit to ride in the meeting. I argued black and blue with the referee for permission to use rider replacement but he wouldn't have it.

Ivan Mauger, Wally Mawdsley and Peter Oakes opened Barrow in the same year, 1972, at the town football club in Holker Street, only 65 miles down the coast from Workington. Wally held the licence as World champion Ivan and Peter, his business partner, were barred from becoming officials by the Promoters' Association. They started off with an open racing permit and then took over West Ham's league licence when the Custom House track closed down early in the season. Peter came up with the idea of calling them the Happy Faces, not one of his best in my opinion. There certainly weren't many happy faces there on the opening night when I went to help, even though I wasn't a member of the promotion.

They had booked the late George Best to do the official opening and, rightly so, it had been well publicised that he was hitting town. The trouble was that he didn't. Ivan had picked him up in Manchester but Best had wanted to go to his hairdresser first so off they went. Ivan waited. And waited. After 40 minutes, when Best had not reappeared, Ivan went in to find him only to discover that he had gone in through the front door and straight out the back. Ivan, as you can imagine, was not amused but, more immediately, the Barrow boys were faced with the dreadful spectre of not delivering their opening night celebrity. There's nothing worse than letting down your punters on the first night.

It was panic stations as Ivan rang Wally in Barrow. He called me to see if I could use my showbiz contacts to find someone to replace Best and keep faith with the Barrow public. They had already suffered the blow of seeing their soccer team kicked out of the Football League to be replaced by Hereford. Getting someone to go up to Barrow at short notice wasn't easy but I contacted the agent of Julie Goodyear, Coronation Street's Bet Lynch, and did a deal for her to come. She arrived in a pair of leopard skin hot pants. She was a big girl and was a huge hit with the fans. So was the meeting because it was a World championship qualifying round and local boy Alan Wilkinson won it. One of the other riders was the late Jimmy Squibb, an old hero of mine.

Racing there wasn't the best because the track was too square in shape and, after a season, Wally, Ivan and Peter wanted to sell. Ivan's racing schedule didn't give him the chance to go there very often while it was a long way for Wally and Peter to travel. I teamed up with George Graham, who was a director at Workington, to buy it from them for the 1973 season. I kept a relatively low profile because I was fronting Workington and it also meant that I was running four tracks.

I had built up my little speedway empire very quickly and it makes me smile now when I read about promoters commenting on the pressures of running just one track. It makes me wonder how I managed. It was probably because I was young, ambitious and a bit daft as well. I had the Owen brothers, Tom and Joe, in the 1973 Barrow side along with Mike Sampson, Terry Kelly, Sid Sheldrick and local boy Chris Roynon.

The chairman of Barrow Football Club didn't like speedway and, at that point, I don't suppose he liked soccer too much either after what had happened to his club. Our race day was Tuesday and one Friday he hired an excavator and started to remove the track. Fortunately, I was in Barrow at the time and soon got to hear about what was happening so I drove straight down to Holker Street. I did my nut at the driver who said he was only following instructions. I bunged him £250 and told him to inform the chairman that the digger had broken down and that he couldn't do any more. It worked and, fortunately, not too much damage had been done to the track and it was repaired in time for the next meeting.

I tried to reason with the football club, but no avail, so I hired a top barrister and he obtained a court injunction to prevent any further damage being done to the track. For a reason I never discovered, the court hearings had to be in London and we could only get an injunction that lasted for two weeks at a time. That meant that I had to go to London every fortnight, meet the barrister and go through the same routine for the rest of season that was a period of eight weeks. It cost a fortune and, by the time those two months had expired, I'd had enough of the place. The track was showing a profit but I'd didn't need the aggravation with everything else I had on my plate and I sold my shares to George Graham. I have to admit that the last time I drove out of Barrow I was the one with the Happy Face!

There was another night when I certainly didn't have a happy face as I left town, more a red one. I have always tried to have a change of clothes in my car boot throughout my speedway career because it's a certainty that, with working outdoors, you are going to get wet on occasions. One night I got a soaking and discovered that I had forgotten the spare outfit so I decided to remove my trousers and drive home in my underpants. I had my Rolls Royce at the time so, as bad luck had it, I was pulled up by the police. It wasn't often the officer stopped a Roller and found the driver in his pants! 'Where's the bird?' he asked. I said there wasn't one and tried to explain my circumstances. The next question didn't help. 'What have you got in the boot?' he demanded. I replied: 'About £2,000.' It was the night's takings and a lot of cash in those days. I can imagine the word burglar coming into his mind but, fortunately, I had a copy of the Barrow programme containing my picture. He told me to bugger off home before I caught my death of cold!

20 – *Kenny Carter: a wasted life*

KENNY Carter was one of the most mercurial riders I have seen during my life in speedway.

Like me, he was a Yorkshire lad. Tough, uncompromising, successful, totally unwilling to let anyone put one over on him.

Unlike me, he was a brilliant speedway rider. He was an outstanding natural talent, aggressive, cocky and a bit wild at times. He had a fantastic will to win. Every race had to be won, even when he rode for me as a kid at Newcastle before moving into the big league.

I knew Carter better than most although, having said that, there were not too many in speedway who wouldn't have been too bothered about getting to know him. Not that he cared. He said what he thought and didn't suffer fools gladly. In my view, there's nothing much wrong with that.

Carter didn't say that much anyway unless it was to do with speedway or business. He'd never sit down and have a pint and talk about a film he'd just seen or a book he'd just read. The kid was a goer all the time and he never seemed to have enough time in a day for everything he wanted to do.

He was a hyperactive, private sort of lad but he had that innate charisma that made people sit up and take notice. You've either got it or you haven't. Bruce Penhall had it then and David Beckham's got it today.

People either liked Carter or they didn't but his personality explained why his death in 1986, when he killed himself after shooting his wife, Pam, made the national headlines.

I got to know him when he was starting his career on Halifax's books and I was promoting at Newcastle where he rode for me as a teenager. Some people found him outspoken and arrogant but we always had a laugh together and hit it off from the first time we met.

Off-track he was a wheeler-dealer, a bit of a Del Boy. He once bought 500 toilets, without seats or tops, but to my amazement he managed to sell the lot and make money out of them.

He even started a sports personality agency and one of the stars on his books was Tessa Sanderson, the international javelin thrower. If he hadn't been a speedway star, there's no doubt in my mind that he would have been a very successful businessman.

He was involved in my England team during the 1980 Grand Slam year but he was basically on the fringe of it and he could never understand why one Yorkshireman, me, wouldn't always pick him, another Yorkshireman, for everything. He was even less happy when I picked a southerner, like John Davis, ahead of him. I told him that his time would come but, unfortunately, it didn't.

I knew Carter throughout his short career and controversy involving him was never far away during my year as England manager. In fact, I resigned from the job because of him even before I'd got to the starting tapes for my first meeting, a Test match against America at Wimbledon as I have related in an earlier chapter.

It wasn't the end of Carter getting me into trouble, though. He was still only 19 when i picked him at reserve for the Inter Continental Final of the World Team Cup at Vojens, in Denmark, and critics said he was too inexperienced for such a meeting. Promoters, fans and the speedway Press all took swipes at me for preferring him to riders like Gordon Kennett and I was accused of a northern bias in team selection.

But Eric and myself felt we needed a reserve who was aggressive and combative, one who would have no respect for reputations if he was sent out to ride which, in the fullness of time, he wasn't.

However, I always defended myself and I also defended Carter when the mud started to hit the proverbial fan. I am sure that it was something he appreciated and locked away in the back of his mind.

If I was right in that assumption, the feelings that he had stored away came out when he broke his leg in 1984. It was put in a cast but he decided he would keep on riding and he asked me if I would act as his manager and adviser for the World Championship rounds.

I thought he was nuts riding with a pot on his leg but if he was going to do it then he needed all the help he could get. So we did a deal and I agreed to look after him.

I was not on his books to advise him how to ride a bike, as Ivan Mauger did in later years, because I wasn't qualified to do that. I was on board to make sure the arrangements ran smoothly, to keep any hassle away from him, and to ensure he knew exactly what he needed points-wise, race by race, to get through the qualifying rounds.

That suited me because I was experienced at reading situations and at pulling the odd stroke here or there when it needed pulling.

The first event was a British semi-final at Oxford and I made sure he had the best spot in the pits. It's a cracking place and many riders will know it because it's still there. There's only room for one bike so I made a few phone calls in advance and arranged for him to have it because of his leg.

We travelled down in the massive motor home that he had bought for a meeting that became infamous because several of Britain's top tabloid newspapers came out the following day and accused many top riders of race fixing.

It was at a time when stories like that about speedway could make two full pages in a tabloid. It was massive coverage but I hasten to add that no accusations were levied on us and Carter qualified for the British Final at Coventry.

We went down again in the motor home and it rained all the way. The weather was dreadful. Carter was still on crutches and, to be honest, he wasn't fit to ride in good weather, never mind conditions like that.

There was water all over the place and the track was like a mudheap. It was so bad I wouldn't even let him come out of the motor home to have a look because he wasn't in a fit state to do it. I told him to stay where he was, to take it easy and keep dry.

Outside it was anything but calm and while Carter sat with his feet up, the rest of the riders were splashing around, looking at the track, holding conversations and generally coming to the conclusion that they didn't want to ride, especially as it was such an important meeting.

Carter, of course, was oblivious to all the aggravation that was going on a few yards away but it finally emerged that 14 of the 16 riders didn't want the meeting to go ahead.

I went back the motor home and said to Carter that if we could get the meeting on we were home and dry – no pun intended!

Virtually all the other riders had seen the track and the conditions and didn't want to ride. They had dropped their heads and didn't want to know.

Carter agreed. He couldn't even walk the track because of the crutches but he said he'd ride it. Even so, he had to make his way to the dressing rooms for the riders' meeting with the referee and the Coventry promoter, Charles Ochiltree.

The senior riders had their say about why the meeting should be called off and then Carter piped up to say he'd race and intimated that the rest of them were wimps in the way that only he could. It was bedlam and, for the first time ever, I saw my old mate Peter Collins lose his rag. He was all for putting a steel shoe over Carter's head and almost had to be restrained.

I hasten to add he didn't but I have never, ever seen Peter as wild he was at that moment. But the other riders were stumped because there was a guy with a broken leg saying he'd ride and the meeting went ahead.

It's almost needless to say now but I'd told Carter that he'd win the British title if we could get the meeting on. We did get it on – and he did win the title! Our policy had worked a treat but we weren't the most popular people around Coventry that night. The Yorkshire lads had pulled a stroke. I suspect some of them realised it and, no, we weren't very popular at all.

Carter scored 13 points with Andy Grahame second and Dave Jessup third. Les Collins, Martin Yeates, Alan Grahame, Simon Wigg and Jeremy Doncaster also got through.

Peter Collins didn't and neither did Chris Morton which meant they missed out on the next round, the Overseas Final, at their home Belle Vue track. I doubt if that improved the general opinion of us. Carter was seventh at the Manchester track, American Lance King winning with a 15-point maximum followed by Australia's Phil Crump and Shawn Moran, another Yank.

That put Carter through to the Inter-Continental final in Vojens, Denmark and one meeting away from the World Final. Again we travelled over in the motor home and, as usual, it was wet when we got there. It's always wet in Vojens.

Nothing special happened in the meeting. Carter wasn't gating very well and, after his five rides, he needed a run-off with Alan Grahame for the reserve spot in the World Final. He lost it. All our earlier efforts had gone down the drain and that was ironic really when you looked back to the wet night at Coventry.

That was the end of me being Carter's manager. He obviously thought I'd got something to offer when he asked me but, in the end, we had nothing to show for it.

He was a brilliant rider and certainly had the ability to win a World Final as I think he showed in Los Angeles in 1982. I've read a lot of comments from Ivan Mauger about how good he was and, of course, it is the ultimate praise coming from him.

Carter was good, exciting to watch and a bit wild at times. He put himself about and upset his opponents but I wouldn't put him in the same bracket as Nicki Pedersen.

It's one of life's great imponderables as to what he would have achieved had he not died in May, 1986 in such tragic circumstances.

I was at home one evening when I got a phone call. I'm not sure who it was from because there were so many phone calls in a short time but

I was told that Carter had shot and killed his wife and then turned the gun on himself. Both of them were only 25.

The policeman who was called to the scene and discovered their bodies was Jim Crossley, a personal friend of Carter, who had lived nearby. He had even travelled with us in the motorhome to some of those World Championship meetings when he helped out in the pits.

My wife, Dot, and I couldn't believe the news. We were in total shock. The phone was ringing its head off. One was from a news reporter of a national tabloid newspaper. I stress it was a news reporter because, generally, I have always got on well with sports writers.

He asked if I was prepared to talk about Carter's career because I'd been close to him for a while and knew him better than most. I said okay. The general speedway questions came along and there was no problem.

Then, after five minutes, he started asking about Carter's relationship with his wife and about certain rumours that were rife at the time. I said I wasn't prepared to talk about anything other than his racing exploits. He tried again and again and I kept saying No.

Then he said: 'We have a big cheque book.' I always remember that. It was the exact phrase. I also remember telling him where to put his big cheque book and put the phone down.

On the day prior to the funeral, the Press were still sniffing about for stories. The funeral could be attended by invitation only and, luckily, my old friend Richard Bott, a well-known journalist, warned me that if Dot and I were planning to go for a drink first, we were to be careful with what we said.

He said the Press vultures would be in the local pubs looking for stories and trying to overhear conversations. And they were. I know that these reporters had a job to do but dirt is dirt. That's all they wanted and I did resent it very strongly.

I did do an interview for Radio Leeds in the churchyard at the funeral but, perhaps for the only time in my life, I stipulated before we started what the questions must be. I said I would only talk about his racing career and that is still the situation.

It was a very, very emotional day. The families had agreed that, despite the circumstances, Kenny and Pam would have a joint funeral and burial service. It was the first time I had been to a double funeral. There were two coffins in the tiny church at Bradshaw, near Halifax, half a mile from their lovely home, a former pub that they had modernised.

The church was packed with 200 relatives and friends with the service relayed to another 500 fans outside. I passed the church recently and, even now, nearly 20 years later, I couldn't bring myself to go in to look at the grave. It was such a dreadful, tragic loss of two young lives.

A myth often grows about people who die young but I think the circumstances in which he died have prevented that. He killed his wife and then himself and that is what people remember.

Nothing justifies that, whatever the reasons, and to this day I won't talk about what was being said at the time because I don't know the true story. But I still find it very difficult to accept that the kid I knew so well ended his life in such a terrible way.

You had to give him credit for his talent on a bike and his business acumen but all that is overshadowed. He'd be in his mid forties now. Wouldn't it be marvellous if we were writing about a rider who had enjoyed a fantastic career?

I wasn't lucky enough to be at the 1982 World Final at the Los Angeles Coliseum when Carter clashed with Bruce Penhall in one of the most controversial incidents in speedway legend.

It's history now, of course, that Carter came out second best in the eyes of the referee after the pair of them had fallen and Penhall went on to win his second crown before retiring on the podium at the end of the meeting to take up a career in films.

But Carter was inches from having the World Championship at his fingertips in that flashpoint moment, only for it to be snatched away. That supports my view that he had every chance of becoming the champion one day because he had so much of his career left in front of him when it ended in such a tragic manner.

I've spoken to Les Collins about the incident but his take on what happened is obviously personal because it cost him the chance of becoming World Champion at the meeting and he had to be satisfied with being the runner-up.

What a lot of people either don't know, or have forgotten, is that Carter was in the race when Chris Prime was killed in a crash at Newcastle in 1978 when I was the promoter.

Carter had finished the race when Prime hit the fence on the fourth corner on the fourth lap. That was another massive low in my career and, I have to admit, I made one of my biggest mistakes as a promoter.

It remains the only fatality I've had and, even now, I remember it as such a simple looking fall, one where you thought he would have got up and walked away. I was first to get to him and I could see it wasn't good.

The track doctor came and got him off to hospital but I received a message very quickly that Chris had passed away.

Bryan Seery, who was secretary of the British Speedway Promoters' Association, was at the meeting and he suggested that I should go on the microphone and tell the people that the rider had lost his life.

It was one of the most foolish things I've ever done as a promoter. We had women screaming in hysterics and people were in shock. Then the police came down, the bike was impounded, the fence was roped off and they found witnesses to take statements. It was awful.

It might sound silly now but what was more awful was driving home and leaving Chris Prime's body in Newcastle. It seemed so wrong.

There was a peculiar twist at the inquest when Newcastle speedway was cleared of any blame in Chris's death. I had to give evidence and was asked if I had any expenses. I didn't want any but claimed for £20 that I was going to give to the Speedway Riders' Benevolent Fund.

They gave me a cheque and it bounced because the coroner died before I presented it. I've still got it.

IAN Thomas with the late Kenny Carter.

21 – Workington: second time around

I HAD been out of conventional speedway for a number of years until Tony Mole brought me back in 1998 after his track at Long Eaton had closed down through no fault of his. Graham Drury was running Long Eaton for him and we travelled down for a meeting at Reading. We went the day before to play in the Speedway Star golf tournament, stayed overnight and had another game on the Monday morning before going on to the match.

Graham introduced me to Tony at the meeting. It was the first time we'd met and I remember it well because I brought him a pint and it took me more than two years to get it back! Tony subsequently telephoned me to say he was thinking of re-opening Workington in the 1999 season. I guess he rang me because of my connections up there through having started speedway at Derwent Park way back in 1970. He asked me about 1,000 questions and while I couldn't answer a lot of them, I had kept a lot of contacts in Cumbria. I told Tony that there were some brilliant people who would be happy to get involved again. He also asked me about the situation regarding planning permission and I told him that we had never needed any.

That seemed the end of it but Tony came back to me a month later to tell me he had an appointment with the board of directors at Workington Town Rugby League club who operated at Derwent Park. He was going up to watch a rugby match against Barrow the day before and would I go with him. I said I would. We met at the game and bumped into several people I knew, including John Walsh who had reported on the speedway when I'd been there and still does to this day. Rumours soon started floating round that I'd been seen back at the stadium with people drawing the obvious conclusions.

It was common knowledge the Workington board was split on whether or not they wanted speedway back. Tony and I had a meeting after the rugby match and agreed that if a deal could be done with the club, and if we got planning permission, I would be the co-promoter and would run it for him as well as being the team manager.

There were five or six directors there when we faced the board, including one character I found to be very unpleasant called John Donovan. I knew he absolutely hated speedway and didn't want it there. He still didn't after we'd opened. He looked me in the eye when we had eventually been invited to sit down and said: 'You are wasting your time. You've got nothing we want.' They were his exact words. I just stared back at him and replied: 'Yes we have.' I paused and added: 'Money.'

There was no answer to that. They did need money and he never spoke again during that meeting. The only times we spoke over the next few years was when there were problems of which I felt he was often the cause.

Another member of the board was Kenny Kirkwood and he started spouting off at the meeting about speedway not being good for Rugby League. I thought that was a bit rich coming from him because he had been my start marshal when I was running the Comets there in the 1970s! Eventually a deal was hammered out, we acquired planning permission and we brought in Tony Swales to supervise the installation of the track. The main contractors were Elliotts who have been brilliant to speedway in Workington. It was all go and we opened in March 1999 with a Del Boy look-alike. I put his picture in the local paper and billed him as a special guest. I got the actual Reliant Robin that had been used in Only Fools And Horses because it was on display at a Cars of the Stars exhibition in Keswick. More than 4,000 paid to come in that night and I reckon half of them still think it was the real Del Boy. He was superb. I remember that meeting, a challenge match against Newcastle, for another reason because we didn't win a race until heat six. But top of the bill that night was Carl Stonehewer who took a second off the track record in that race and set us on the way to a 47-41 win. He had ridden for Tony at Long Eaton in 1997 but, after the closure, he had spent a season on loan at Sheffield. He enjoyed riding there but said the money wasn't brilliant and, once we had got planning permission, I invited him and his dad, Bryan, to come up for a look. We hadn't started work on the track and I could have killed him when he made his first comment: 'It's going to be like Exeter.' I wasn't too impressed because I remembered Carl had once been asked how to improve speedway and he had replied: 'Drop a bomb on Exeter.' He certainly didn't fancy it at first. Then I took them to a place called Oily Johnnies, a pub I always used for my lunch when I was up there. I made Carl an offer but couldn't persuade him to sign so I asked him to think about it. We met again a fortnight later at Birch Services on the M62, near Rochdale, and that time we did a deal. That piece of business was, without a doubt, the most important thing I ever did for Workington speedway.

Stoney is a legend in Cumbria. He became so popular up there that I even negotiated for him to switch on the Workington Christmas lights one year and there aren't many speedway riders who are asked to do that. He even got paid for doing it. We had a good working relationship over my six years up there – for most of the time. We had a couple of spats in that time but realistically that's not bad in a sport like speedway.

The best publicised one was in 2003 when it was decided by the Elite League promoters that Premier League riders could double up in both divisions. Belle Vue promoters John Perrin and John Hall contacted Stoney, without my permission, before I'd got home from the conference. It was a totally illegal approach. When I spoke to Stoney I told him I didn't have a problem over him doubling up but I did have a problem in doing a deal with John Hall over the financial aspect of Belle Vue using a rider who was contracted to Workington. Perhaps Belle Vue thought there wasn't a problem because the doubling up principle had been agreed but I certainly had a problem over another club using my rider for nothing.

The situation dragged on through the winter. Perrin, Hall and myself couldn't do a deal and, all the time, Stoney was becoming more and more agitated over the danger of missing out on a considerable number of extra meetings. I might not have been too keen on him doubling up because he was my top man and what would have happened to Workington if he'd been injured racing for the Aces? But I defy anyone to show me where I said that he couldn't double up. What I said was that he could go if terms were agreed but, in the end, we were forced into a deal because the Promoters' Association laid down set fees, which we had to adhere to. So Stoney got his season at Belle Vue and we got our fee, even if we weren't allowed to negotiate it. But feelings had run very high over the situation and it wasn't finally settled until Tony Mole, myself and Stoney had a meeting at the pre-season Press Day. At one stage it had looked very much as if he wasn't going to ride for Workington.

The other bust-up came after the double points rule had been introduced at the start of the 2004 season. It could be used if a side had fallen ten points adrift but riders weren't to be paid for six points if they won a doubling up race from the gate. If they started 15 yards back and had to take more risks then I would pay them extra money and that was only fair. But somebody had planted it in Stoney's head, and I don't know who it was, that he should be paid for double points when he was nominated as a tactical reserve.

He was told that wasn't the case but he came into my office one Saturday night, with his dad, Bryan, and said he wanted paying for double points or he wasn't going to ride. I told him not to be silly. There was less than an hour to the start of the meeting and not only did he leave my office, he left the stadium. I told people that if he didn't return, he would never put his leg over a bike for the Comets ever again and I meant it. But he did come back. And he never did get paid double points. It could have been the end of his Workington career but, just the same as after the Belle Vue bust-up, bridges were built and we are still the best of mates, which is good.

Stoney became the first Premier League rider to qualify for the World Championship Grand Prix in 2000 after finishing third in the Challenge final at the end of the previous season. That was at Lonigo, in Italy, and when he was preparing for his last race he asked me what he needed to do. I told him to get his head down, his backside up, and go like hell. Then he asked what would happen to Workington speedway if he got through because we raced on Saturdays, the same night as the Grand Prix meetings. I told him to go out and ride and let me worry about the fixtures. He qualified in what was one of my proudest moments in a special night. There were so many fans out there in Italy to support him that they had cleaned Workington's foreign exchange shops out of lire and more had to be rushed in. Simon Stead later qualified for the Grand Prix as a reserve in 2003 and had a couple of GP meetings while he was riding for Workington.

A lot of the old staff came back when we re-opened including Tony Jackson and Rolly Hughes as well as some cracking new ones. Tony and Rolly are great Cumbrian characters who helped me so much in a number of ways. The people of West Cumbria are a different breed. You get the odd nutter, like you do anywhere, but 99 per cent of them up there are wonderful. When we didn't do well they gave me some stick but I never had a problem with that. They are the kind of people who will support a rider as long he's trying. It's when they think someone is taking them for a ride that they make their feelings known.

I could write a book on Workington alone. I flew to Sweden to sign Peter Karlsson, the rider we called our Peter Karlsson and not PK from Wolverhampton. He was an absolute gentleman.

When he signed I arranged a publicity stunt to fly him in by helicopter. I didn't say from where so people might have assumed it was coming in from Sweden. It was, in fact, coming all the way from Maryport which was about three miles down the road. I publicised the fact a helicopter was coming in but another Rugby League director, Wilf Harrison, told me I couldn't do it. He said it might damage the grass. I told him it was coming in anyway. Again he said No. I replied that I'd advertised it and I wasn't going back on the decision, even if the helicopter had to hover three inches above the pitch while Peter jumped down.

Anyway, it came in and landed and it was extremely spectacular. We were in contact when it took off so we got everyone looking for it as a dot on the horizon which grew bigger and bigger. The helicopter belonged to a company called Cumbrian Seafoods which was based in Maryport. The matter didn't finish there, though. A month later Wilf Harrison asked me what official permission I'd obtained to land a helicopter at the ground. I told him to go away. I wasn't having it.

Nigel Pearson was the stand-in announcer the night Peter left the club. He got Peter, Stoney and myself on the mike and all three of us were crying. He had decided to call it a day because he'd had some bad knocks and he had become a father. Also the travelling had got him down because he lived out in the sticks and the air schedules meant he had a four-hour wait en route.

My relationship with the majority of the Rugby League board wasn't totally harmonious. I once got a rollicking from them for pulling a stunt when the Bobby Roberts circus was in town. The club used to rent some of their land to the circus for the week. I went to see Bobby because I knew he'd got two elephants. I asked him if we could borrow one if we publicised the circus and he agreed. We were running the Premier League Pairs on the Saturday night and I wanted the Workington duo, Carl Stonehewer and Micky Powell, to ride round on the elephant in the interval.

We put a big flag on the elephant and the two riders climbed up. They weren't happy because they were a long way off the ground. I had Geoff Powell walking behind with a shovel and a bucket. The whole thing went down a treat with the crowd but it didn't with the Rugby League boys. They said I should have asked permission to bring an elephant onto the track, even though they had rented their ground to the circus. I found that type of thing very frustrating because all I was doing was trying to put on a show.

We won a lot of honours at Workington over my six years there, both individually and as a club. Stoney won the Premier League Riders' Championship twice, and we won the League Pairs and Fours competitions several times. The only thing I never won was a seven-man competition and I spent enough years trying. I had a five-year spell initially in Workington and then a six-year stay. It is my greatest regret that I never managed to win a full-team event.

Workington's crowds often exceeded those enjoyed by Elite League clubs and we had three civic receptions over the years. One of them was held by a very colourful mayor called Mel Pettitt, who was well known as Mystic Mel. We also had another great character in Dr Andrew Butler, the best track doctor in speedway as far as I am concerned. He is now the top medical man at the Speedway Control Bureau. He's very strict and when I approached him in our first season at Workington I gave him a copy of the rulebook which lays down certain medical requirements. He came back and said it was no good. I told him I hadn't written that part of it.

Anyway, he sacked the Workington St John's Ambulance people the first night. I asked him what we were going to do next. He said it was my problem. So I went to the Whitehaven branch and he wasn't thrilled with them. I told him that if I sacked them there would be no speedway because there weren't any more St John's branches in that part of the world. I suggested we brought in a nurse as back-up and he agreed to that. He was extremely hard work in the first year he was with us and that's how it should be. He has become a very good family friend and I'm proud to say that.

He once went out of his way to visit Stoney at his home in Denton when he was struggling after a crash in a Grand Prix in Sweden. The bloke is brilliant and a lot of riders have much to thank him for.

On a lighter side, I guess every track has its own traditions and one of Workington's concerned new riders who had come from overseas. When they went to ride at the Isle of Wight for the first time, I would go up to them at the interval and say: 'We're in trouble. We can't get back to England tonight.' I think the first one to experience this leg-pull was Peter Karlsson and he asked why. I told him the Channel was flooded. They all believed it. I'd warned Stoney that I was going to try it on Karlsson who went to tell him of the problem. Stoney kept a straight face and said: 'The same thing happened when we were here last year.'

Kauko Nieminen fell for it as well. He was another lovely lad who I signed from Finland and he made friends with Karlsson, being as they were both from Scandinavia. They were pulled for speeding on a motorway one night and PK told Kauko just to speak in his own language. The police weren't having much joy with one talking in Swedish and the other in Finnish. In the end they said: 'To hell with it. Too much paper work.'

I went over to Helsinki to watch Nieminen ride and negotiate a deal. To my surprise he told me we needed to get a train to the track. He said it would take just over an hour to get there but, after 20 minutes, he said we'd have to get off at the next station. I asked him why. He told me we were going in the wrong direction. But we got to the track in time and I still signed him.

Tony Mole has a personal terms contract with every rider at his tracks. It was something he had devised before I joined his operation but it's very good – Stoney refers to it as the contract which says you can't pass wind in the pits – but it does give me the right, as team manager, to fine a rider, who can appeal to Tony if he is not happy about it.

I've only used that power once when I fined Grant MacDonald, who I found to be a very disagreeable person. One night at Workington he felt that our start marshal, Kenny Fearon, was giving him a hard time. He punched Kenny in the bar after the meeting, splitting his nose and breaking his glasses. All hell broke loose and although I was on the way home by then, I knew all about it because my mobile phone never stopped ringing. It was totally unacceptable and when I got back I rang Grant for his version of what had happened. He admitted he was in the wrong so I told him he was to pay for Kenny's new glasses and that he was being fined £250. That took him aback but I told him that if he wasn't happy he could put in a transfer request. He said he couldn't afford the fine so I told him he could do the same as if he'd been in court and pay so much a month. I said it would be £50, unless he wanted to appeal to Mr. Mole. I informed Tony who felt I'd gone over the top, but MacDonald never appealed and the money went to the Speedway Riders' Benevolent Fund.

The lad was a handful and perhaps I should have sacked him. On another occasion I was driving through Workington and saw a poster advertising a hen night with male strippers. It said: 'Also starring Grant MacDonald, the Workington speedway star.' I wasn't having any of that because, although I'm not a prude, speedway is a family sport so I rang him up and told him that if he went ahead with it, he was out. He said it was up to him and I agreed. But I said it was up to me whether or not he stayed in the team and the next time I drove past the poster it had been deleted. He went at the end of the season anyway.

He was the only rider I fined but another I fell out with was Mitch Graham and, unlike MacDonald, that really hurt me. Mitch had ridden for me at Hull and Workington for many years and had been very good for Workington speedway when Tony and I were setting it up. But he decided to get involved with the promotion of stock car racing at the track with Wilf Harrison and Steve Rees. It was a total flop and only lasted a season but it wasn't acceptable to Tony Mole or myself for him to have a foot in both camps. He wanted the best of both worlds but he couldn't have it and Tony dismissed him.

Tony Swales was another character who was indispensable at Workington. I referred to him as the Henry Kissinger of the speedway world because it was virtually impossible to fall out with him. When I was having all my problems with the Rugby League people, I used to ask Tony to try to sort it out for me. I'd go in feet first but he'd be much more tactful. He was known as the track curator but he was so much more than that and a massive asset to the club.

Workington was an outpost and we were proud of the fact but it didn't mean that hardly anyone knew we existed. Far from it. We attracted a lot of TV coverage and Channel Five came to do a documentary with us. The working title was Birds, Bikes and Blokes and that put me off immediately because I suspected a stitch-up.

They were grand people and they stayed with us for the best part of a season to do a fly-on-the-wall documentary. Every time they came it rained but it didn't put them off and it went out finally as a one-hour film. We got a fee of one pound for doing that but the publicity was priceless. I agreed to that as long as they gave me a copy of every inch, every second they filmed – and did that get me in trouble? They accepted that condition as long as I didn't show any of it commercially so I've got film at home of a back wheel going round and round for eight minutes. There's about 18 hours of it and the problem was that it was uncut. I'd watch it at home and Dot would keep saying: 'That's you swearing again.' It was too easy to forget they were there and the language can get a little fruity at a speedway meeting. After it had been transmitted, the TV critic of The Times no less gave it a brilliant review. He said he'd turned it on expecting a load of garbage and had really enjoyed a very good programme.

One of my fondest memories out of thousands at Workington was the night I took my official farewell after the 2004 season before taking over at Belle Vue. The news I was leaving had broken just before the end-of-season dance and I'd had a bet with John Walsh, the Comets' Press Officer, that I would get booed because I was leaving. When it came to my turn to give my thank-you speech I said how much I'd enjoyed my six years there, on top of the five years of my first spell at Derwent Park. I wished the club every success in the future and I couldn't believe it when more than 250 people stood up to give me a five-minute ovation. I'm not an emotional person but I was then and I'll never forget that. In fact, I was so emotional I bought John Walsh a pint of Guinness.

I organised a couple of sportsman's dinners while I was at Workington to raise money for cancer charities and I hope no-one will be offended if I recall the second night in particular because there was a room full of people crying with laughter. The first one raised £6,000 and the next £4,500 so I was quite happy with the results.

I booked Bernard Manning for the first and he was supported by one of the Grumbleweeds who went under the name of Graham Grumbleweed Walker. Manning was brilliant although I couldn't repeat much of his material here.

My top of the bill for the second dinner was comedian Mick Miller with an impressionist from Liverpool. My problem was that the first dinner had been so successful that it was a tough act to follow so I decided to book a third artist. His name was Mr Methane. I'm not sure if I should say that he farted to music but, there you are, I've said it anyway. Perhaps I should say that he passed wind to music.

I had worked with him before at Sam Wella's fun pub in Birmingham. I was doing my Unrideable Bike and Electric Chair routines with my son, Lyndon. We'd been contracted for three days, along with Mr Methane, but we were paid off after one because no-one turned up.

Mr Methane was a delightful guy from Macclesfield. He did an hour's act but I told him I only wanted 15 minutes so he said he would fire darts as well as playing Flight of the Bumble Bee and Blue Danube. I'm serious although I did wonder later if the first tune should have been Bum of the Flightle Bee!

Mick Miller, who had never seen the act before, and I had tears rolling down our faces and so did everyone else. Then he came on dressed like a green Superman and wearing a mask. Mr Methane lay on a table, drew up his legs behind his head and blew out the candles out on a birthday cake. I don't think he was invited to many silver wedding parties!

Then came the finale. I had to find someone to take part and I had just the man in mind. Mr Methane had a big balloon which he strapped on the top of the head of my 'volunteer' from the audience. Then he put a dart in a pea-shooter and applied it to the power source with the victim kneeling nervously in position. Mr Methane got the crowd to count down 10-9-8 and, when he got to zero, he fired the dart which burst the balloon with a loud bang. It brought the house down. And the man wearing the balloon? My co-promoter Tony Mole.

22 – BSPA: *they made me see red*

WHEN I came back into speedway at Workington in 1999 the British Promoters' Association had a dress code for club officials and I had nothing against that. After all, wasn't I the team manager who had made the England riders wear blazers when we achieved the Grand Slam in 1980?

What I didn't like was the colour red and the dress code insisted on different jackets for different jobs. A promoter would wear bright blue as a rule with a navy blue one for formal occasions and team managers had to wear bright red. All of them had badges and I was all for the principle because I have never been to speedway in my life without wearing a collar and tie. Very few people do even that these days so we have officials wearing all kinds of casual gear and I don't think that's right.

But I didn't like the bright red blazer one bit. It was compulsory to wear it but I thought it made me look like a lollipop and I was determined, by hook or by crook, to get out of it as the 2000 season approached. I rang Sharon and Angela, who run the BSPA office in Rugby, at different times and said I wasn't keen on the red blazer. I asked them both if I could use my dark blue one when I was team managing and they said no. I had to follow the rules and be fined if I didn't.

I sat down to think of a solution. I came up with the idea that I was allergic to red. I contacted Dr. Mahapatra, a friend and very eminent psychiatrist whose work includes giving opinions for the Home Office. I did have a history of eye problems, and still do, so when I explained the situation to him and I asked him if he could write me a To Whom It Concerns letter saying I was allergic to red, he agreed.

I phoned Angela, with a little pleasure I have to admit, to tell her that I'd acquired medical evidence about my allergy and that I couldn't wear red. It would be fair to say that she found it hard to believe and who could blame her? She told me to send a copy to the BSPA which I did. Then I phoned to ask if she would circulate a message to all the referees instructing them that I wasn't to be fined for not wearing red. She said: 'No, just carry a copy of the letter.'

I did but it got to the stage where almost every referee wanted a copy for himself. Perhaps they had never seen anything like that before! I finished up running off about 20 copies so they could have one each to save. And that's why you will never see me in a red jacket.

Having said that, I do think promoters and team managers could be smarter these days when they are in public. What I can never understand with the BSPA is that when we go to a promoters' meeting we all wear our navy blue jackets, white shirts and ties. We sit there round the table looking at each other dressed in our speedway best. We seem to dress up for each other but not when we are in front of our public.

Several people at the BSPA took the mickey out of me and asked how the hell I'd got out of using the red blazer. I just told them to get a good consultant!

Dr S B Mahapatra

Harrogate Clinic, 23 Ripon Road, Harrogate, HG1 2JL

Telephone: (01423) 500599

                                                                          Fax: (01423) 504100

25 February 2000

                                                                          SBM/SB

TO WHOM IT MAY CONCERN:

Re: Mr Ian THOMAS (3.1.42)
         30 Halstead Drive
         Menston
         Ilkley
         LS29 6NT

This is to state that the above-named is known to be over-sensitive to bright red objects including clothing. I have therefore advised him to refrain from wearing bright red clothing or to be in close proximity with people who are wearing such garments. This is to prevent over-straining his eyes after he had surgery for cataracts in both eyes and treatment for inflammation of the eyes (iritis).

S B MAHAPATRA FRCP FRCPsych DPM
Consultant Psychiatrist

---

23 – It's a knockout

RAIN and champagne, perhaps even a tear or two, ran down my face. I was the happiest man in speedway. Belle Vue had just won the 2005 Knockout Cup in front of their own fans to complete a fantastic recovery from the brink of possible extinction.

It was a great night, not just for the City of Manchester but also for speedway as a whole as the great club was not only up and running again, but running at full speed.

I couldn't know it then but, within a month, I was to endure three of the most miserable days of my 35 years as a promoter.

The thought of British speedway without Belle Vue, or even as a Premier League track, didn't bear considering but those were options facing the World famous Aces until Tony Mole put his money on the table and bought the club lock, stock and barrel from John Perrin at the end of 2004.

Tony had put me in charge as co-promoter and team manager so the cup success, as well as finishing top of the Elite League table, was payback for him, reward for the fans who swelled the attendances by 60 per cent and my answer to the knockers who had criticised my team selection.

It was also a massively deserved reward for the best team in the League who would have added the championship but for an injury at a crucial stage of the season to our No. 1, Kenneth Bjerre.

But all that elation evaporated in a flash at the annual conference of the British Speedway Promoters' Association in Tenerife. The side I had built and nurtured was destroyed by a decision I bitterly opposed to reduce the cap on team strengths from 42.5 points to 40. I had feared it may go down to 41 but 40 was a disaster.

I sat long into the night in my hotel trying to find the answer to a question I knew had no answer. I had to reduce the overall team strength by six points, more than I'd ever had to do before in my career. It was miserable work because I knew all the time that it wasn't a case of reduction; it was a case of destruction. I had to take apart a team that had graced British tracks at home and away and entertained millions with their performances on live TV.

I felt I was doing speedway as a whole no good, never mind Belle Vue. And, to compound my feeling of misery in Tenerife, a place I don't like anyway, was that I knew that sooner or later I was going to have to tell three riders – nearly half the team – that there was no place for them in 2006.

Jason Lyons and Andy Smith were desperate to stay and so was young Aussie, Rusty Harrison, who had ridden for us when his commitments with Premier League Edinburgh allowed. He was close to deciding to join Belle Vue on a full-time basis but I had to phone him in Australia and tell him to forget it because his average was such that I couldn't fit him in. We had even bought Smith's contract from Coventry and have promised him an overdue testimonial in 2006, even though he won't be in the team. Lyons was known as Mr. Belle Vue because of his long service, having ridden for the side every year bar one since 1992.

One thing I have learned in my years in speedway, as you will gather as you read this book, is that you must always move on and, despite what I still view as a wrong decision to water down the strength of the Elite League, I remain optimistic about the way speedway and Belle Vue are going.

The Knockout Cup win was the pinnacle of the year and the annual conference the low point but there was so much else happened that pointed to a good future.

Belle Vue, once more, are part of the fabric of one of Britain's greatest sporting cities. That was shown by a Lord Mayor's reception, increased media interest and the accolade of being invited to the BBC North West Sports Personality of the Year dinner at a plush Manchester hotel. I was thrilled that we were even sent two tickets and so was my rider, Simon Stead, who bought his first dress suit and went with me. But that was nothing compared with the moment the three nominations were announced for Team of the Year, which were European champions Liverpool, Championship winners Wigan and Belle Vue speedway. Liverpool won it, of course, but I was so proud that we were mentioned in the same breath. It proved that the Aces were upwardly mobile again and it is a trend that I am determined to maintain.

We had come a long way in the 12 months since we had taken over. To be given the chance to manage the world's most famous speedway club for the second time at the age of 63 was a very special moment. So how did it come about? I was sitting comfortably enough in my sixth season promoting and team managing the Workington Comets for Tony Mole. They had been the best supported club in the Premier League and we hadn't done too badly results wise. I was part of a successful set-up, I was enjoying the job up there in Cumbria and there seemed little reason to change it.

I knew Tony had tried to buy Belle Vue a few seasons earlier, without success, and I was also aware that he had been having provisional talks with John Perrin towards the end of the 2004 season. Tony rang me one day in October and said: 'If you had the chance of continuing at Workington or moving to Belle Vue, which would you choose?' Within seconds I replied: 'Belle Vue.' No more was said. Tony came back to me two or three days later to say that he had bought the famous Aces, subject to contract. My three-year contract to run Workington for him had expired so we sat down and sorted out another three-year deal. But, this time, it was for Belle Vue.

Many people have asked me why I chose to move and I can understand the question because I loved it at Workington and most people knew that. Home race days were a joy from the moment I left my house because I had the loveliest drive through the Yorkshire Dales and the Lake District to get there. I did it that many times I virtually got to know the sheep – and there were some good-looking sheep! When I arrived I was involved with a great team, on and off the track, and I thought the world of the fans up there. I still do. But I also felt I'd taken the Comets as far as I could and that I needed a new challenge. And they don't come much bigger or better than Belle Vue. I'd have been a fool to turn it down and, fortunately for me, the people up in Cumbria appreciated that.

When it was announced that I was moving from the Premier League to the Elite, one promoter said to me: 'You are moving from a league of gentlemen into a den of vipers.' I'd love to print his name here, but I can't. I would also add that while I don't necessarily agree with the remark, I know where he was coming from. You need to have your wits about you in the Premier League, but even more so in the top competition. At least I'd operated there before so there were a lot of old faces still around with a few new ones mixed in.

My first job was to put the team together and that didn't get off to the best of starts. When I arrived at my first Elite League promoters' meeting at Rugby, I was presented with a copy of the Coventry Evening Telegraph saying that Jason Crump was about to join the Bees. That was a load of rubbish for starters. Belle Vue knew nothing about any such move and, without divulging details of the meeting, I soon put a stop to that nonsense. If Coventry had any thoughts before the meeting that they were signing Jason, they were thinking about something else by teatime. I didn't even have to meet Crumpie to do a deal. It was sorted in a couple of phone conversations.

Wheels and Deals

The points limit was set at 42.5 points so I set off to work up to that target and the next rider I signed was Jason Lyons, a Belle Vue asset who had been at Poole for much of the previous season before finishing it at Premier League Newcastle. There was a major dispute over the average that the Management Committee gave him and my views over that have been listed many times. It cost us the chance to sign Ricky Ashworth, who went to Poole. I haven't forgotten.

I wanted Simon Stead who was a Workington asset and had ridden for me there for two years. He had made the decision to move up to the Elite League before Tony bought Belle Vue and we had already given Wolverhampton promoter, Chris Van Straaten, permission to talk to him. Simon had ridden a few matches for Wolves at the end of the season and had done well but, once Tony had got hold of Belle Vue, obviously I wanted him at Kirkmanshulme Lane. Chris tried very hard to get him and I didn't blame him. He offered us Swedish rider Fredrik Lindgren in exchange but I wasn't interested and I am still sure that I made the right decision, even though Lindgren also had an excellent season. I was delighted when Simon accepted our terms because he is a massive talent who will go a long, long way in speedway, even though he has made the British World Cup squad already. I like Simon and I like his family who are speedway through and through and lovely people. I also like his mechanic who revels under the name of Jetwash Johnny, which was given him at Workington by Carl Stonehewer who reckons he is brilliant at washing bikes.

Then I did a deal with Joe Screen, who had started at Belle Vue as a 16-year-old and had been with the club the previous season on loan from Eastbourne. I'd dealt with him in a few ice meetings at Telford and, again, it was deal done after a couple of telephone calls. I like Joe who has a great sense of humour and is one of speedway's big characters.

Next was young Dane Kenneth Bjerre, another Belle Vue asset. He speaks good English and that helped me to tie up a quick deal on the phone and then came 39-year-old Andy Smith, who I landed even more quickly than that. It was a controversial signing with some fans, probably because of his age, and he couldn't believe he'd got a job in November instead of the following March after his experiences of previous seasons. Smudger had suffered the rough end of the stick for long enough and I think that he responded well to take the chance Belle Vue gave him. The amount of riders he passed, particularly at Belle Vue, was unbelievable and he had a wonderful season. He proved wrong the critics who thought I had made a mistake so I was as pleased for myself at his success as I was for him. But, I have to say, he used to infuriate me and the other riders by being last to the tapes on every occasion, something which he has done all his career. I asked him why it was and his answer was: 'By the time I get there, everybody has stopped digging.' Fair comment, Andy.

I gave the final place to Steve Masters and, after eight meetings, he was finding it hard going so I took the tough decision to drop him after a match at Poole. I brought in Rusty Harrison and Krister Marsh who doubled up with their Premier League clubs, Edinburgh and Isle of Wight. The team was sorted out by Christmas and that was the only change I made all year.

In the meantime, Tony had appointed Belle Vue legend Chris Morton M.B.E. as Commercial Manager while we retained some of the established staff and replaced others. One of the best signings I made was Richard Frost, who I have known forever. He was one of the media men who became a friend over the years and I asked him to be our Press Officer, a position I regard as vital at any club but one that Belle Vue had never filled before. Richard, also the speedway correspondent of the Manchester Evening News and Speedway Star, is one of the old school and he has done a brilliant job for us. One of his first tasks was to publicise a fans' forum at the stadium soon after the takeover and I was concerned about the response to the new promotion and to myself because I'd had a couple of spats with the club during my Workington days. So I drew a lot of encouragement from the fact that the meeting attracted more than 400 fans. To add sparkle to the proceedings, I flew in Kenneth Bjerre from Denmark, without the fans knowing, to sign his contract and that proved a popular move. I have always been a great believer in giving people surprises.

Apart from putting together a successful team, I saw my main job, especially in the early months of Tony Mole's takeover, as letting the public of Greater Manchester and beyond know not only that Belle Vue speedway still existed, but there were real moves in hand to take the club back to the top. Via Richard Frost, the coverage has flowed with great support from local TV and radio stations as well as the Press and speedway websites.

Next on the agenda was sorting out an opening night attraction. The first thing in my mind was the guy who blew himself up in a coffin but then I came up with the idea of drawing together the club legends who won the World title while riding for the Aces. If that were possible, we would open with the Peter Craven Memorial Trophy in respect of the club's late double champion. I managed to get them all, Ivan Mauger, Ove Fundin, Peter Collins and the current champion, Jason Crump. What a line-up! To round it off perfectly, Peter Craven's widow Brenda, now Mrs. Leat, also agreed to come over from her home in Ashton in Makerfield in Lancashire.

We were also working hard to market the Aces and as well as attracting a superb main sponsor, in Fonestyle UK, we also brought in heat sponsors and sold more advertising space. It would be fair to say that Belle Vue was on its knees when we took over and, if I couldn't have increased the crowds from what they were, I would have packed up. In fact, I should have been sacked if I couldn't have improved the situation I inherited.

Colin Meredith came on board as track curator and Tony Mole spent an absolute fortune on a new circuit and more than 250 metres of drainage. More than 20 meetings had been lost to the weather in the previous season but Colin did a superb job and we lived up to Tony's pledge that no meetings would be called off if it didn't rain after 5pm.

All we wanted for the opening was a dry night. The World champions were there, we had a cracking crowd and they saw Belle Vue riders fill the first three places with Crump the fitting winner. We were up and running. What amazed me was the amount of former riders who became regulars throughout the season. Riders like Peter Williams, Peter Collins, Ken Eyre, Jim Yacoby, Eric Broadbelt, Chris Morton, Taffy Owen, Carl Stonehewer and Bill Powell.

The season went well with the team top of the table for most of it as well as staying in the running for the Knockout Cup, which the club eventually won for the first time in 30 years. The vital statistic which gave me the biggest boost was that the crowds kept increasing with old fans coming back and new ones coming along for a look. Just let anyone try to tell me that publicity doesn't work.

Media coverage increased with the crowd size and, what was equally pleasing, was the fact that so many top riders made a point of congratulating us on the racing surface. We staged a qualifying round of the World Under-21 championship, having got the track back on the International Motor Federation roster, and have filed away a copy of the report from the FIM Jury that described the track as 'near perfect.' We were getting things right and that was proved when we were asked to stage the 2006 Championship of Great Britain.

My target at the start of the season was a top four finish but we went even better, taking top place in the Elite League. In most sports, you are champions if you finish top at the end of the season but that's not so in speedway. We had to go into the play-offs and had a home semi-final against Eastbourne, on the strength of being top, and we landed a two-leg final against Coventry. History shows that we lost but, in my view, the reason for that can be explained in three words: No Kenneth Bjerre. He had been badly injured in a crash in Denmark shortly before. For a long time afterwards people asked me: 'What did you get for finishing top of the league after 36 matches?' The answer to the question, amazingly, is nothing. Not even a packet of crisps and a pat on the head.

Even so, the second leg of the final at Kirkmanshulme Lane was unforgettable, despite the disappointment. We had a big crowd with fans queuing for two miles to get to the stadium. When was the last time that famous old Hyde Road had seen a speedway queue like that, I wonder? It was the fifth heat before they were all admitted but we couldn't delay the start because the match was live on TV. In addition, we sold out of a special souvenir programme that did the club great credit.

Losing was hard because I had believed the championship was ours all year until Kenneth was injured. Up to that point, if I could have chosen the side I wanted to meet in the final it would have been Coventry because we had won there twice, once in the league and once in the Air-Tek Trophy. At least we still had the Knockout Cup to go for and the boys and I managed to lift ourselves for the final. We accepted that the title had gone and we started again to make sure we had something to show for a year's work.

I don't like picking out riders because this is essentially a team sport but I will mention the performance of Jason Lyons in both legs of the final because he was superb. He also made me take my biggest gamble of the season in the second leg at home because he had run two lasts, one because of a bike problem, when I gave him an extra ride against Nicki Pedersen. It was a do or die decision and I'm told there was a groan from the crowd when my decision was announced. Fans thought I was barmy but I had to do it. My reasoning was that he'd only had one bad race and that if we were going to win the cup, I had to get him scoring points. I showed confidence in him and not only did he win the race, he was unbeaten by an Eastbourne rider in his last four rides. I could have finished with egg on my face but Jason wasn't bothered when I told him he was going out for that race. After all, we had one thing common. We're both old pros!

I have deliberately avoided talking about scores and scorers in this book because it is not the purpose to fill it with statistics. But I will mention that we lost the first leg of the final at Eastbourne by a couple of points and took the trophy by winning 53-37 at home. It was a great night, another big crowd, which was capped by a deserved triumph, and a victory that was nowhere as comfortable as a 97-83 aggregate suggests. There was a trophy in our cabinet in the first season, the first since the League championship in 1993, and it felt good. I was pleased for everyone, the riders, Tony Mole and especially the long-suffering fans. One of them, a pensioner and season ticket holder called Alex Broadhurst, came from Chingford, in north London, on public transport for each match. He used buses, a train, an inter-city coach and a lift from a mate and it took him the best part of 16 hours to do a home match so I was very pleased for him as well.

We asked Allan Morrey, who had retired at the start of the season after 61 years' service with the Aces, to present the trophy to Jason Crump. I always felt Allan had been poorly recognised by the authorities for his remarkable contribution to speedway and this was some recompense because he rang me the next morning to say it had been the best day of his life. I was pleased to see that the Speedway Riders' Association recognised his work shortly afterwards when he was presented with their Special Service award.

We had ridden 28 home matches by the end of the season, as against around 20 the previous year, and then agreed a new three-year deal with our landlords, the Greyhound Racing Association, who have been brilliant. And they must have been happy with us because, in the past, they had operated on 12-month deals. I rarely went to Belle Vue before we took over but people tell me there's a buzz around the place again, which is very rewarding to hear. We won't be resting on our laurels, though, because there are things that aren't right and some of those we may not be able to fix. But there are others we can rectify as we continue our quest to make sure that the Legend of Belle Vue lives on.

Apart from the two Premier League riders we used, we didn't have a guest rider all season and, in all those 28 home matches, we didn't have anyone from either side taken to hospital which is unbelievable.

A few things in particular have stuck in my mind about the 2005 season. There was Jason Crump's 21 points in the first leg of the play-off final at Coventry which was a World class performance. Then there was the occasion when a VAT man and referee insinuated I was a liar on live TV, a World class rider attacked me in a phone box, again on live TV, Manchester City manager Stuart Pearce brought his entire squad to a match in a bonding exercise and the lovely Sophie Blake introduced their goalkeeper, Nicky Weaver, as a Manchester United player, again on live TV. I'm told that Manchester United's former England star Paul Scholes is a regular visitor.

All in all, our first year in charge could have been much worse. I've got a wonderful view across the Yorkshire Dales to Ilkley Moor from my lounge and I enjoyed some time to relax during the winter looking out from my rocking chair – with the Knockout Cup on the little table next to me!

JOE Owen, winner of the Speedway Star Best Pairs at Hackney, with former model Samantha Fox.

24 – *Elite League tracks and promoters*

WHEN John Berry wrote his highly successful book, 'Confessions of a Speedway Promoter', he commented at some length about me and not all of it was complimentary. I promised him that my turn would come. Now it has.

Berry was a successful promoter at Ipswich and an England manager in the years leading up to my magical season in charge in 1980 when England won the Grand Slam.

He e-mailed me several months before his book was published because it contained a chapter about me. He asked me if I'd read through it because it would be cheaper than getting a lawyer to do it. I told him that he could print the lot without any fear of comeback.

I never liked going to Ipswich. For a start it was such a long trip although I suppose Ipswich people probably said the same about going to Workington. Also, I never took a winning side there until Belle Vue won at Foxhall in the 2005 season. And, thirdly, John Berry was the promoter.

I disliked him intensely. We just didn't get on together. He was a bloke who didn't give the impression of enjoying life very much. He wasn't big on smiles. In fact, I've been told that he had to leave his local pub at six o'clock in the evening so they could start Happy Hour!

But, I have to say, he was a very good speedway promoter until he packed in and went to live in Australia and I enjoyed reading his book.

It was very cleverly done with each chapter being named after a song. Mine was The Silver Tongued Devil and I by Kris Kristofferson. For some reason there was more about me in that book than there was about his partner, Joe Thurley. Some of the stuff he wrote about me was factually correct and, as far as I'm concerned, some of it wasn't. But it was a damned good read.

I once took a Workington side to Ipswich in the early seventies and he got two heavies to carry me out of the pit gate about 15 minutes before the start and dump me. We'd had a row about the make-up of the teams. As I was being carted out I shouted back to my team: "Follow me." They did.

I told Berry that we were all staying out there until he let me back in so it was up to him whether or not he had a meeting that night. He let me in and it went ahead.

When he and Joe Thurley were running tracks at Doncaster and

181

Ipswich, they came up to Workington with Doncaster and, at the start time, they had only three riders in the stadium. I could have asked the referee for them to be put on a charge but they promised me that the other riders were on the way and I decided to wait, rather than drop them in it with officialdom.

Pretty damned good of me, or so I thought. I felt that one good turn deserved another and there was a vote coming up at the Promoters' Association that I wanted to go through for my own benefit. I cannot remember what it was about but I said I wouldn't press charges over them arriving late if they would vote for me at the BSPA meeting. John said that would be no problem.

Eventually, we went to the meeting. I put up my proposal, it went to the vote and both their hands went up against me. They double-crossed me and that taught me a lesson.

But, despite everything I've said, speedway is a better place for John Berry having been involved in it. I've no doubt about that and, even in view of my personal feelings about him, I've no problem in saying it. I never saw him as a great personality in the sport but he had a very bright speedway brain and people could learn from the way he did things.

Things have changed at Ipswich since he left. John Louis, a former star rider, is in charge down there now. I like John but he's a bit deaf and I'm a lot deaf. If you ever hear us in conversation, we say 'Pardon' a lot.

I seem to have been going to Eastbourne forever. It always seemed to be hostile. I used to arrive early, which I always do anywhere, and have a coffee in the caravan with the late Charlie Dugard and his son, Bob.

I'd sell them a bit of gear that I'd got on the go, 70-piece gold cutlery sets were always popular, and then it was away with the social side and on with the racing. That's when the hostilities started.

Mike Sampson once ran me over and floored me on the track; I never got on with him. Another time I was dragged away by a member of the track staff and I thought he was going to hit me. I shouted: "Hey, what have I done?" He told me that a pensioner with a walking stick was standing behind me with a knife and he thought he was going to stab me. Bob Dugard still remembers that.

Then there was the infamous incident when Tom Owen, one of my top star riders at Newcastle, threw a teapot at the referee who, if I recall correctly, was Lew Stripp. Tom felt he had been excluded unfairly from a vital race and stormed off to see the official. His box was up a ladder, it still is, with a tea stall underneath.

Tom knocked the door but couldn't get in so, in his frustration, he put the pot through the window. He was charged with bringing the sport into disrepute. I decided to defend him at the Speedway Control Board and he was found not guilty but I don't know how I did it. It may have been something to do with my love of watching court cases. I go when I can because it's good entertainment and cheaper than the pictures. Seriously, I marvel at the language of the barristers and would love to have seen the late George Carman in action. I've watched cases for the prosecution and been utterly convinced that the defendant was guilty. Then I've watched the defence and been as sure he or she was innocent. The ability to blind people with a load of bull is so important and, perhaps, that is how I got Tom off The Case of the Flying Teapot.

We used to do a round trip to ride at Canterbury on a Saturday and Eastbourne on the Sunday. A couple of coach loads of Newcastle fans used to come and we'd stay over in Eastbourne after the Canterbury match.

I enjoyed going to Canterbury because I'd have half-an-hour with the one and only Johnnie Hoskins before the meeting. That was always a great pleasure and a privilege. When the meeting was over I'd take all the boys, except for one, into the bar for a drink. The other used to have his way with a female member of Johnnie's staff and then we'd set off in convoy to our Eastbourne hotel.

Bob Dugard is still there doing the track but not promoting and Jon Cook runs it now. I've got to say that until I came back into the Elite League with Belle Vue at the end of 2004 I wasn't too keen on Jon. But since then I've learned more about him and have very much changed my opinion. Jon has a very acute speedway brain, he runs a good show at Eastbourne and we get on well.

It's also a much friendlier place these days. At least I haven't been in danger of being stabbed since I've been going back there with Belle Vue.

The only problem I've had down there as team manager of the Aces was at a meeting in 2005 when it got a bit hairy at a meeting when Chris Gay, the VAT man, was the referee. But that was just a problem between him, a member of the Eastbourne track staff and myself.

I've said before in the book that my word is my bond and that I've employed the world's greatest riders like Ivan Mauger and Barry Briggs without a written contract. So I was very unhappy that night when Gay took the word of the Eastbourne Clerk of the Course in a dispute over a team change and, in my opinion, insinuated that I was lying. I had a furious row with Gay after their official had told him I wanted to replace Andy Smith with Simon Stead in a race.

I had discussed the possibility with the riders but decided not to make the change and stick with Smith. When it was announced we were making a change I went on to Gay and told him it was incorrect. I felt that the Clerk of the Course must have overheard our conversation discussing the situation.

I had a furious row with Gay but he ruled in favour of the home official. I was incensed and told him he was calling me a liar. It infuriated me more than I can say. What made it even worse for me was that the incident was covered live on Sky TV. I bet they loved it but I thought it made speedway look like a joke when the referee and a home official could tell a visiting team manager what he could and couldn't do with his own team.

Peterborough opened the same year as Workington in 1970 and, as Graham Taylor would say, did they not like us at the time. They were run by Allied Presentations and applied for permission to run at the same time as I did. We were both turned down by the British Speedway Promoters' Association for entry to what was then the Second Division of the league.

We both appealed to the Speedway Control Board. You had to pay a £10 protest fee but Allied Presentations subsequently bought the licence from the defunct Plymouth track for £1,000 so they were in. I had to go through with my £10 appeal, won it, got my £10 back and joined the league for nothing. I might have smiled a bit!

But that wasn't the end of it because Allied, a powerful organisation with several tracks, were clearly rattled they'd paid £1,000 for what had cost me zilch and I was a one-man band newcomer. A member of the consortium, Danny Dunton, came up to me shortly afterwards and said I would need the help of Allied in the future and that I should give their company £500, half of what they'd paid Plymouth. I gave him a one-word answer beginning with B.

Peterborough have had a number of promotions over the years and I do like the latest set-up. Colin Horton has only been in there for five minutes with Neil Watson and Trevor Swales.

I've always enjoyed going there. People may know that I won the Four Team tournament there with Workington and Newcastle but what they probably won't know is that I raced there in a grasstrack meeting before it became a speedway stadium. Happy memories, indeed.

Wolverhampton have been promoted by Chris Van Straaten for

around 20 years so he must be doing something right. I met him for the first time when he came to Workington as team manager of Stoke in the 1970s and we have had our share of disputes over the seasons.

On that night he complained about the height of the safety fence but I had the answer to that – a tape measure with a foot (30cm) cut off the end. We checked the fence with my measure and, believe it or not, it was fine. We had a few spats but we were both new in those days and we were learning.

When I came back into conventional speedway, after running the Telford ice shows, CVS had just been elected as chairman of the Promoters' Association and he did an above average job during his reign. It's a thankless task and I learned how to read him like a book after watching him in charge for a few years.

If there was a particular discussion at a promoters' meeting, which wasn't going his way, he would extend the debate in an attempt to swing the vote. I don't blame him for that because I've done the same thing myself. He had a little more opportunity to do that as chairman but I wouldn't knock him for it. I would deem it to be one of the perks of the job.

He has had Pete Adams as his team manager for a long time and, between them, they put on an absolutely first-class show. Mind you, I've had my moments with Peter and he rubbed me up the wrong way in the 2005 season when Belle Vue were at Monmore Green for a live Sky TV match.

I had just bought a designer coat, which cost me about £350, and I was rather pleased with it. Pete was there in is his bright designer anorak when we met with interviewer Sophie Blake. At the end he commented to the watching world that it was nice to see that there was an undertaker in the Elite League. We went off air and I didn't have a chance to fire back at him but, as luck had it, Belle Vue were on TV at Swindon a fortnight later so I wore my undertaker's coat again. I was determined to get my own back, and I think Sophie suspected it.

I don't know what she asked me as her first question but, like any good politician, I diverted it and said: "I'm wearing the undertaker's coat I had on two weeks ago when we buried Wolverhampton and one of the Adams family."

Ever since, I've kept a £20 note in the coat pocket and if anyone else makes any sarcastic comments about it on TV, I'll hand it over and tell them to go to Oxfam and smarten themselves up.

Arena-Essex are operated by big Ronnie Russell and he is a formidable bloke. I've heard our fans chant 'Are you John Perrin in disguise?' at him but if he told me tomorrow was New Year's Day I'd say okay.

One of Ronnie's biggest claims to fame, which has nothing to do with speedway, is that he was once a hero in frustrating an attempt to either kill or kidnap Princess Anne, now the Princess Royal, on March 20, 1974. Her Royal Highness and Captain Mark Phillips were returning to Buckingham Palace from an official engagement when a car swerved in front of their chauffeur-driven limousine on the Mall, forcing it to stop.

The driver of the other car fired several shots, as he demanded that Princess Anne leave her car and go with him. Ronnie was driving along the Mall when he saw the gunman trying to open the door of the Royal limo. He went to assist and, in the on-going confusion, Ronnie punched the man in the face.

The man ran off as more police arrived and he was apprehended. Ronnie was awarded the George Medal by the Queen for his bravery, which proves that he is a big man in more ways than one.

I always enjoy going to Purfleet. I know a nice restaurant for a meal. Then I stop at the top end of the car park for a couple of hours' sleep before the match and that keeps me fresh for the drive home. It's also nice to bump into people like Alf Weedon, the long-time speedway photographer and former England star Dave Jessup. He always reminds me of how I left him behind in Poland in 1980, when I was the England team manager. He had lost his passport after we had won the World Team Cup.

It's such a shame that the crowds aren't bigger at Arena. It is regarded as a trick track for away teams but the surface is always top notch. The downside of visiting there is that you have to travel on the M25, the biggest car park in the world.

Poole are probably the best supported track in the United Kingdom under the promotion of Mike Golding and Matt Ford and managed by Neil Middleditch. I was in Poole for a full day in 2005 and I was impressed with the way they advertised the speedway.

I've always been one to search out different ideas for publicity and advertising but they sprang a new one on me when I was coming out of a multi storey car park. The barrier was down to force you to stop while you paid but staring straight at you on the barrier was an advert for Poole speedway.

You just couldn't miss it so everyone who parked there must have been made aware of the Pirates. People may think that is a small and insignificant point but, as someone who fully realises the value of promotion, I was very impressed. It is that sort of attention to detail that makes a track successful.

Matt and myself have had several disagreements and, during one of them, he came out with a cracking one liner that I shall use myself when the opportunity arises. He referred to me as having a very selective memory and I thank him for the compliment.

Poole are a track with a win-at-all-costs attitude, which, within certain parameters, is not a bad thing. Mike and Matt run the best-supported track in the country so who am I to knock it?

Matt, my wife Dot and I were among the guests invited to Barry Briggs' 70th birthday bash in Coventry where we stayed in a hotel and we were bussed to John Harrhy's golf club for the function. We started talking about the ruling over what Jason Lyons' average should have been at the start of the 2005 season when he returned to Belle Vue from Poole via a spell in the Premier League with Newcastle.

I had worked on one figure in my team-building plans and was then told it was another that was higher. That meant I couldn't sign highly talented local lad Ricky Ashworth without breaking the 42.5 points limit on team strengths. I always thought I'd been stitched up and said so.

The talk grew into an argument and Dot jumped in to say we were bang out of order behaving like this on the way to Briggo's party. She was right. It was a social event and we shouldn't have been having a row about business. So we shut up.

When we arrived at Harrhy's place, I went to look at the table plan and, of course, we were on the same table as Matt Ford. I thought I'd better square things. I went up to him, shook his hand and said: "Why don't we let bygones be bygones for a couple of hours?"

His reply shook me. He said: "You don't have to apologise." That set me off again. I said: "I'm not xxxxing well apologising. I'm just saying let's forget the job for a couple of hours." We did, and we had a great night.

Relations were fairly easy after that because we didn't see much of either other. But I must say that I was absolutely delighted that Poole failed to match Belle Vue's proud record of winning a hat-trick of League championships because that was top of their agenda for 2005.

I know Coventry pipped us for the League title, and we had to be satisfied with the runner-up spot, but I liked the place in the old days and I like it now. It holds a lot of memories for me, not all of them good.

There was the Kenny Carter incident in the British Final and the match when Hull lost the 1979 League title there. I've already talked about those incidents but there was also the night when Carl Stonehewer won the Premier League Riders' Championship there as a Workington rider when I was running the place.

It has always been a well-supported and well-run track. Avtar Sandhu owns it now and while I have only met him a few times, I have found him to be a very polite man. He is obviously very clever.

My old pal Colin Pratt promotes it and he tells a good tale. He has some great Tony Mole stories and if you get the chance ask him – he might tell you a few. I also go back a long way with joint team manager Peter Oakes. He's one of the best in the business and he can pull or stroke or two.

The only person I can't get on with at Coventry is Jeremy Heaver – or is it Weaver? I can never remember but, fortunately, I don't have to deal with him. In my opinion he has been in speedway for five minutes and, in my opinion again, he has caused disruption.

Jimmy McMillan, my former No. 1 at Hull, is the machine examiner at Coventry and it's always a pleasure to see him down there.

In the old days the Ochiltrees were in charge for years and going there was a different kind of experience. Mrs. Ochiltree, who ran the front desk at the office, always greeted me with the words: "You aren't looking very well today Ian." If you ever got past there and through the two doors to Charles Ochiltree's pad you were very privileged – either that or he wanted something!

I've already referred in the book to going to Oxford in the 1980s when I was Kenny Carter's manager and it's a stadium I've always enjoyed visiting. I have to say, though, that rightly or wrongly in my view, the stars of a speedway team are its riders but I'm not sure that has been the case at Oxford in recent seasons.

It would be easy to think that the star there appears to have been former promoter, Nigel Wagstaff. In 2005 Oxford were probably the only track in speedway to have a photograph of their promoter on the front cover of their programme as the main feature, with the riders in the background. But everybody to his own.

Swindon is a great racing track, now under the control of Terry Russell and promoted for him by that great character Alun 'Rosco' Rossiter, who features elsewhere in the book. He's a bubbly lad who is easy to wind up but, like all Terry Russell tracks, it is well run.

25 – Premier League promoters and tracks

LIKE any other promoter in speedway, I have tracks that I prefer to go to and promoters who I prefer to deal with ahead of others. Some people I like, some for one reason or another I don't.

I know that people will say the same about me because I've rubbed a few of them up the wrong way over the years and I guess there will be more to come.

Promoters should try to work together for the benefit of our sport as well as for the well being of their own tracks and businesses but it would be naïve to pretend this always happens.

I'm as guilty as the next man for putting my own interests first and, on occasions, for getting even when I reckon another promoter has pulled a stroke on me. Here, in no particular order, I would like to run through the Premier League tracks and promoters I have come to know best in recent years.

I have always enjoyed going to Rye House to listen to Len Silver's stories. He's what I would refer to as a proper promoter. He isn't a man who just opens his turnstiles on a race night and expects people to come in.

He loves his sport and is never short of a tale. Anyone who gets the chance to sit down with Len for half an hour should make sure they do. Either way, Rye House is a smashing place to go for speedway because he knows how to run an excellent show on a smooth track.

My favourite Len Silver story is about when he used to be a door-to-door salesman. He'd buy anything and then go out to sell it. He once had some small, hand-held fire extinguishers, which he gave another salesman to sell for him.

Unfortunately, he didn't have much success so Len went out armed with a jar of lighter fuel that he'd spray on his jacket after knocking on a door. When the occupant answered, Len would set fire to himself and then put it out with his extinguisher, which promptly sold like hot cakes.

He's a character, he loves his sport and few people have a greater knowledge of how it works. We've had our run-ins over the years but speedway will be a poorer sport if and when he retires from it.

I've got a lot of time for Newport promoter Tim Stone. He built Hayley Stadium virtually single-handedly from scratch and not many one-man bands have done that in speedway. We get on quite well but

I do keep telling him that if he had a corner shop, instead of a speedway track, he wouldn't open it just 30 times a year.

That's what he does with the speedway but he ought to think of other things to do with the facility that will bring in revenue. He could try things like Christmas markets, a pop concert or even a lap dance club. If he extended his social facilities he could get so much more out of his stadium.

I pulled a stroke over him once when he had two riders with identical averages. It was a matter of which one was rated the higher for rider replacement purposes because that would decide which one would get the most rides.

I said it was the guy who was higher on the last official green sheet averages but he said he had a letter from the British Speedway Promoters' Association giving him permission to say it was the other one.

I didn't fancy that and asked him to show me the letter but he didn't have it with him. I knew that if I'd argued the toss with the referee an hour before the meeting, he might well have gone Tim's way.

But every day the BSPA have a designated member of the management committee on duty and I reckoned I'd a better chance of getting the verdict I wanted if I telephoned him. He can only be approached if there is a dispute within 30 minutes of a meeting starting and, irrespective of whether his ruling is right or wrong, there is no appeal against it.

I knew who was on duty and I won't name names. But I felt I could convince this particular person to rule my way and he did, even though Tim had a letter saying the opposite. Tim was subsequently proved to be right but we won by two points and there was nothing anyone could do about it.

But, to be fair to him, he took it well and treated it as a learning experience. He won't fall for the same stroke again and may pull it off on someone else, if he hasn't already! I hope the guy prospers because he deserves it.

I don't like the venue at Berwick and I dislike the promoter, Peter Waite, even more. I've been there many times over the years with Workington and I always seemed to have trouble.

He incensed me so much once at a Premier Trophy match at Workington that, when it came to heat 15, I went up to him in the pits, told him he was trespassing and had to go. So he went.

The last time I went to Berwick with Workington I went into the football social club at the back of the stand for a drink after the meeting with my wife, Dot, and Tony Mole, my promoter, and rider Claus Kristensen.

Peter had built a new compound just outside the pit gate and when we came out it was locked up with just one car in it. Mine. He would have known who it belonged to and it was obvious where I was so it wouldn't have been a problem to send me a message to move it if it was that urgent.

There were two Berwick fans with us, who also weren't too keen on Peter, and they were prepared to pull down the fence so I could get off home. I told them not to do that. Claus rang Peter to ask him to come down to let me out and I'm told his answer was not printable in this book. I wouldn't have liked to kiss him anyway - anywhere!

He came down eventually and let me out. I never said anything at all. What I will say now is that I've bought two sets of wheel clamps from Halfords and they will be used at an appropriate time.

I liked going to Glasgow as much as I didn't like going to Berwick. Part of the reason was that Workington seemed to win there a lot. The track is always good and promoters Alan Dick and Stewart Dickson always put on a good show.

Brian Sands fronted the previous promotion but he was unable to attend once when we went up there. His team manager was there but rules state that at least one promoter must be present at every meeting to be the official promoter

Bob rang me, said they would make sure the show would run smoothly but asked if I would be the official promoter, even though I was with the away team. I said it wouldn't be a problem but little did I know!

The one downside of going to Glasgow was the machine examiner they had at the time. He always gave us grief. I think the word is jobsworth. This meeting was no different because he found something allegedly wrong with two of my riders.

But this was my time. I invited him to go away. He said that if I spoke to him again like that he'd report me to the promoter. I said: 'Listen, sunshine, today I AM the promoter. Go away.' I have to admit I enjoyed that after all the stick I'd taken from him.

We always found Edinburgh to be a trick track although the surface was always well prepared by Alan Bridgett, nephew of the late Bill Bridgett who a lot of us will remember with great affection from his days promoting at Wolverhampton.

The stadium has seen better days but the consortium who run it, fronted by John Campbell and Alex Harkess, deserve a lot of credit for keeping speedway operating in Edinburgh, not just at that stadium but down at Meadowhall.

I've had a few run-ins at meetings with the Monarchs because we used to go two or three times a year and John knows the rulebook inside out. I had a nose-to-nose bust-up with him once and that's very difficult when you look at the difference in our sizes. He's a big fellow.

Hull, my old track, have had several different promoters in recent seasons. I'm biased but I preferred the old Boulevard Stadium to Craven Park where the Vikings ran for the last few years.

It's an unusual track because it's narrow and there's not much room for passing as I know only too well. But the riders seem to stay close, it always appears as if there is going to be some overtaking and, strangely, the racing looks good.

I've always enjoyed going there since I finished as the promoter. My old mate Eric Boocock used to run the side and it was part and parcel of matches between our sides that we gave each other a lot of stick.

I used to introduce him as Albert at Derwent Park and apologise to the fans that Eric had been unable to come. It was a laugh, a wind-up because everybody in speedway knows Eric. Or so I thought until a referee told me he didn't have any knowledge of a licensed team manager called Albert Boocock.

Sheffield is a cracking stadium and a great racetrack where Neil Machin and Malcolm Wright run a very professional show. I think I can talk a bit but Neil could captain England for talking.

There is a big home advantage because it's a big, fast circuit, one of the best in the country. They rarely get beaten at Owlerton because a rider needs to have his engines specially prepared for it.

That's why it gives me extra pleasure to say that the last two times I've been there as a team manager, I've been in charge of the winning side. I took Workington in 2004 when we gave them their first defeat for six years and then in 2005 with Belle Vue.

Stoke is a far cry from how it used to be because the surface was awful until the stock cars moved out. Carl Stonehewer, my captain and No. 1 at Workington, used to swear that there were rats living in the visitors' changing room. He made a formal complaint to the stadium bosses to that effect but, I have to say, I never saw any.

It has benefited from a parting of the ways with stock cars as promoter Dave Tattum now has sole charge of the speedway and the greyhounds. The facilities and track at Loomer Road are a great deal better than they used to be because we used to have a lot of problems with the surface.

The place would be much better still if Nigel Crabtree wasn't there as team manager. He always seems to be shouting, waving his arms about and going up and down the ladder to the referee's box. He's a nuisance.

On the other hand, Buster Chapman works like a Trojan at King's Lynn and I've got all the time in the world for him. The stadium isn't the King's Lynn of old but he's improving it and it's all credit to him.

I wasn't laughing at the time but Buster once had a fall-out with Rusty Harrison's mechanic when I was there with Workington. I got between them to prevent any serious fisticuffs and, when I looked on the Internet the next day to see what it said about the match, the headline said Chapman and Thomas in big bust-up. That'll teach me to be peacemaker.

I loved going to the Isle of Wight because we did it on a round trip, going to Exeter or Reading on a Monday and then drive down to Portsmouth docks, stay the night and take an early boat over.

The lads would go to the track, do their bikes and then have a day on the beach if the weather was all right. It's a lovely island and going there was like a mini break.

Dave Pavitt, one of the promoters in the consortium over there, is a real character who likes to pull a stroke if he can. At one meeting his captain was Craig Boyce and mine was Carl Stonehewer. We needed maximum points from the last heat to force a draw and we just had to win the toss for gate positions. The situation was simple: Win the toss for the one and three gates and we'd the chance of a point. The alternative: Lose the toss and lose the match.

Dave came over to Carl and myself and said: "Let's spin the coin." He flicked it up, Carl called correctly and we won. Great. Then 'Pav' said we'd have to do the toss again because his captain wasn't there.

I said: "Not likely. It was your idea to do it." But he wouldn't have it and I certainly wasn't going to back down and do it again. To my amazement, he called in the referee. He was a new guy who had just qualified and, to my disbelief, he told us to spin again after we had both put our sides of the story.

Again I said: "Not likely." Or something like that. Fortunately for me, referees Robbie Perks and Tony Steele, the guy I think is the best in the sport, were not only spectators at the meeting but were standing yards away. I asked the match referee to speak to them for their view before he implemented his decision. He came back and said: "The result stands."

The referee went back to his box so we could get on with the race and Dave, knowing he'd failed to pull a stroke with the coin, came out with the classic line when he said: "Thomas, you always were a tosser." I can't remember if he said anything after my lads took full points from the race and we got the draw.

Most teams hated going to Exeter and that applied to Workington in particular. They've had some World class riders there over the years in Ivan Mauger, Scott Autrey and Mark Loram. It's a track that takes a lot of getting used to so visiting riders, in particular, didn't like it.

When Carl Stonehewer was made captain of Workington, a journalist once asked him what he would do if he could make one change to improve speedway. He said: "Drop a bomb on Exeter."

We went all the way down there once and the floodlights went off. Incredibly, they tried to illuminate the track by putting cars on the centre green with their lights on but it didn't work so we had to go all the way home and go back again.

I took Workington there in 1999 and, as usual, it was a damage limitation exercise. At Exeter, the team managers usually stand just outside the pit gate near the fourth corner. On lap two of the first race, they were getting maximum points by a mile and Stonehewer was third. He came past and shouted to me: "I'm not damn well going out here again tonight."

I'm deaf in one ear but I still heard him because he was going so slowly. When he came round on the third lap I shouted back: "You damn well are." From that point we ignored each other but he did go out for a total of five rides.

The next time we went there the track was unbelievably rough. Carl went out for the parade on a trials bike for a lap and nearly fell off. I'd nipped out to a shop and bought a model of Bob the Builder, the kid's toy. It was bendable and I fixed it to the front of Carl's bike with his hands over his eyes.

I always had trouble with the Clerk of the Course at Reading. I liked Pat Bliss and Chris Shears, the former promoters, but it didn't stop us having problems. Carl and Anders Henriksson have a history that goes back a long way. I've seen a video of Stoney chasing him across the centre green at Sheffield with a shovel in his hand. Fortunately, someone stopped him.

That was before he rode for me but there was a near riot on one trip. They clashed on the fourth corner when Henriksson ran into Stoney. They both came off but Stoney jumped up and started pummelling him. All hell broke loose on the centre green. There were about 30 of them fighting.

I was trying to get Stoney out of the way but I was getting hit and thought: "To hell with this" and left them to it. I'm no fighter. I stood there watching with one of my riders, Kauko Nieminen. He's a lovely feller, an extremely quiet lad who couldn't punch his way out of a balloon. They had a mascot who was dressed in a full lion outfit and this lion suddenly came up to Kauko and said: "Do you want a fight?"

It was a serious situation but I just fell about laughing. It was so funny and so was Kauko's unprintable answer. Not many people would have said that to a lion and lived to tell the tale!

Stoney was fined £1,000 and given a two-year suspended ban. The whole team needed a security escort out of the stadium. We were going on to the Isle of Wight rather than driving back north and I told them not to stop for anything to eat until they got down to Portsmouth.

Reading has an indelible place in my memory for a much happier reason. They were in the British League back in 1982 when I was team manager at Belle Vue and we won there to virtually clinch the championship.

Somerset have a lovely little stadium just off the M5. The surface is always superb but Eric Boocock, who ran it for a season, is of the opinion that the straights should have been made longer when it was built. He feels it would have made the racing even better.

There may be a good reason for it but I don't think Friday is their best race day because it's not a good night to be coming down the motorway. It's just an observation but they might be better off running in midweek. It's like going round the M25 to Arena-Essex. If you cop for a traffic jam, you've had it.

26 – Not a lot of people know this

THERE are a variety of different events and stories in my life which, to quote legendary actor Sir Michael Caine, not a lot of people know about.

Some are speedway related while some aren't. They don't really have a natural slot in the chapters of this book but I would hate to go to print without relating some of them so I have assembled them here in no particular order.

The first one in particular I love and I cannot say how much I'd like to be able to name the rider involved. I think and hope you'll understand why it's not possible. One season, in the not-too-distant past, the Sports Council dropped in at a Workington meeting to do a random drug testing which applies to any sport these days. They tested the seven riders of each side for alcohol prior to the meeting and all of them were clear. Then they told us that they would pick any two from each side after the meeting for a random urine test. And that's where this one rider was hit by the panic button although not for the reason you would naturally assume.

One of the two Comets riders picked for the drug test came up to me after he had been handed the dreaded bottle. He looked anxious and said: 'I knew it would be me. I'm a bit worried.' I asked why and couldn't believe the answer. He told me: 'I'm on a promise tonight with my girlfriend – and to make sure it's a good night I've taken Viagra.' I told him: 'I can see why you are worried – it is a performance enhancing drug!'

I told him to go to see the track doctor, in fact there were two present that day. They got out the relevant book which would say whether or not there was anything illegal in Viagra. I was hooting with laughter while the rider stood there looking anything but passionate until Dr. Butler, our track official, gave him the all clear. The rest of the story has remained secret.

Our rider was the one with the red face on that occasion but another time the embarrassed expression was mine. Oxford rode at Workington in an Inter-League challenge match in 2002 and, prior to the following season, Newport promoter Tim Stone rang me to ask my opinion on Danish youngster Niels-Kristian Iversen, who had ridden against us. He had been offered Iversen on loan by Oxford and my immediate answer was: 'Don't touch him with a barge pole. He was crap.' Then doubts started creeping in. Had I been a bit hasty? Finally, and thankfully, I called Tony Jackson, the Workington programme editor, and told him I'd warned Newport off signing Iversen. He said: 'Why? He won two races our place.' I jumped back on the phone and told Tim to sign him, which he did. Iversen ran a near ten-point average for Newport and now he's a Grand Prix rider.

A tale that involved me, but one which I only discovered years later, concerned a skint student from Leicester University and, to be honest, I didn't remember the incident when he recalled it years later. It happened when I was promoting at Newcastle and the student came up to Brough Park on a bus to take in a meeting which was then rained off. He had paid to come in so he had a rain-off ticket valid for any one of the next three meetings. Obviously, we didn't know each other but he came to see me and explained that, as he was a hard-up student, he wouldn't be able to afford to come back so soon and could he have his money back instead of the rain-off ticket. I said he could. Then I asked him how much he'd paid for his bus fare and gave him that as well.

And who was that student? None other than Tony Steele, who is now correctly regarded as the best referee in world speedway.

One aspect of the Telford Indoor Ice show, run by myself and Graham Drury, is that it has become a weird tradition that we have a rider in the field who never gets paid. Before you run off with the wrong idea about us, let me add that so many riders want to take part at Telford they would do it for nothing and we could, in fact, have more than one freebie in the line-up every year. It started off accidentally but it was something that very nearly came back to haunt us one year. It was the first year that a rider called Phil Morris rode at Telford and he was the only one who wasn't getting paid. I doubt that even Phil knows this story in full but, as it happened, he took to the ice like a natural. He did very well riding for England in the afternoon show and then we came to the British Open championship, the big event, in the evening. Phil shocked us all by winning his first three of five races and, suddenly, Graham and myself realised that we could have a champion who wasn't getting paid while everyone he had beaten would be getting an envelope. Press Officer Richard Bott came to tell me that the media boys had found out and that it wouldn't do much for our credibility if the story came out with the headline: British Open champion doesn't get paid!

I spoke to Graham and the upshot was that he went to the pits and did a deal with Morris before he rode another race. And, of course, we were then made to pay by Sod's Law because he finished last in his final two races! We never cease to be amazed by the amount of riders who want to take part at Telford and we have a queue every year. Even to this day, there is a rider at Telford who doesn't get paid because he would prefer that to missing out.

I don't know if odd things happen only to me but once I had to hold up a meeting at Workington for 20 minutes because a taxi driver turned up with a sick teenager in the back. I asked him why he'd come to Derwent Park rather than hospital. He said it was because he knew there would be a doctor at the speedway. Our track doctor, Andrew Butler, gave her emergency attention while waiting for an ambulance but I thought that was a pretty poor commentary on the state of the NHS if the best chance of finding a doctor in Workington was to take a patient to a speedway match.

I found myself with a most unwanted record when I was running Hull because I employed an odd job man who turned out to be one of Britain's biggest mass killers. He changed his name from Peter Dinsdale to Bruce Lee in 1979 after his hero of the martial arts films but, throughout the 1970s, many people died as a result of fires he had started. He pleaded guilty to 26 charges of manslaughter at Leeds Crown Court in 1981 but this figure was subsequently reduced to 15 when the conviction involving eleven elderly men at a residential home was quashed. I used to pay him small amounts to sweep up and I sacked him a few times which, on reflection, was probably a dangerous thing to have done.

Still on the dark side of life, Dave Younghusband, the former Halifax star and my team manager at Newcastle, was once quizzed as a suspect in the Yorkshire Ripper murder. He has a Geordie accent and that was a line of enquiry for a long time because of tapes that had been sent to George Oldfield, who was the policeman in charge. Poor Dave was one of thousands of Geordie boys who who were questioned at the time and I know he was very worried.

I realised during one season in particular at Hull that certain turnstile operators were on the fiddle. I spoke to a CID inspector about it and, as a result, we videoed them at it over a period of six weeks and prosecuted seven. They had taken from £15 to £200 and were ordered to pay it back, some of it at 50p a week. People asked me why I bothered with the prosecution when it wasn't really worth it but my purpose was not financial but purely and simply as a deterrent to others. It's an on-going problem and you can't always tell if it's happening. I can't mention names but I'm told that even high-tech new stadiums aren't fireproof from the fiddler. I'm not suggesting that every turnstile operator is at it but there are bad apples in every barrel and it just so happened that there were rather a lot of them at Hull.

My money-making ventures haven't been limited to speedway and I have mentioned some of them already. In addition, during my first spell as the Workington promoter in the 1970s, I had a go at putting on a few variety shows while, in more recent times, I have staged gigs with bands from the 1960s which have proved very popular.

But back to Workington. I was always looking to explore other avenues of income and have to admit that my efforts met with mixed success to say the least. I once booked Acker Bilk and his band to appear at a dance in the Coronation Hall in Ulverston, near Barrow, and 18 people bought tickets. I didn't need an accountant to know I was on a big loser. That wasn't all because I'd got him booked to play at Workington the next night. It's what you might call reinforcing failure because the advance sale there was a dozen.

Acker was a lovely bloke and he felt very sorry for me that my venture with him hadn't worked out. I felt quite sorry for myself actually because, financially, I'd blown my brains out. The band had a barrel of Somerset cider with them and while they were playing Stranger on the Shore at Ulverston, I was drowning my sorrows with it in the wings. Acker and I sat down with another glass or two after the show and he was happy enough to take half his agreed fee and give Workington a miss. What a gent.

Did it put me off? Not likely but, on occasions, I wish it had. I moved to the bigger venue of the Market Hall, in Carlisle, which has gone now. It held 1,500 people and acts I put on there included the Syd Lawrence Orchestra, Norman Wisdom, Gene Pitney and Moira Anderson. Strangely, the one act that I thought might struggle to make me any money was the most successful of the lot and that was Moira, the lovely Scottish singer.

Gene Pitney was on a UK tour and I bought one night of it. How it works is that the main promoter brings an act across and books as many show as he wants. Then the free nights are made available for other promoters to buy in to the tour and that's where I joined the fun. I just couldn't see taking a big name like Gene Pitney to Carlisle being anything but a surefire winner but those Cumbrian folk just didn't agree. He sold out everywhere in the country, apart from Carlisle, and I had paid him £1,500 which was a mountain of cash in those days. He was doing two houses for that so I had 3,000 tickets to sell but we played to just 600 collectively. He was an absolutely delightful man and one of the smartest I've ever met. His act was brilliant, it went down very well with the audience – and cost me a fortune!

Norman Wisdom came next. I thought he was a comic genius and still do. People might think his brand of humour is an age thing but not too long ago I was talking to Workington riders Carl Stonehewer and Rusty Harrison who both said that one of his films was their all-time favourite. Norman was a bit dearer and I hadn't learned my lesson because I booked him for two houses as well. I was in the theatre waiting for him and I knew it was him coming along before I could see him properly. It was the walk that told the story, even off stage. Norman was a lovely man as well. He asked me about the ticket sales and I told him they were lousy.

That really concerned him because he didn't want to perform in front of poor crowds and he asked me to start telephoning nursing homes and hospitals to see if I could give away tickets and fill the place. I wasn't prepared to go along with that and he went back to his hotel, leaving his stooge to set up the act. I didn't like him at all which perhaps explains why I can't remember his name.

I was sweeping the stage when this guy came in. I recognised him because I'd seen him on TV. He brought in the props and asked: 'Will you be here tonight?' He obviously thought I was a stagehand but I said I would. He had a machine with a boxing glove on it and it kept punching Norman. I helped him get it into the wings and he told me that when he said 'Where's that tiger' during the show, I had to push it on stage. So the show started with a little over 200 people in the hall. Despite the fact I was on another financial beating, I was in stitches because he's so funny but the stooge was a different kettle of fish because I'd found him rude and obnoxious. When the 'Where's that tiger' line came I just stood there. He gave me a look, and I mean a look, before saying it again - and again.

The third time I gave a V sign, which the public couldn't see, and he came and collected the contraption himself. He was in a fury. After the show he came up to me and demanded: 'Just who on earth do you think you are?' I replied: 'I'm the daft bastard who is paying you and don't ask me to push it on for the second house.' Norman Wisdom came over and asked what had happened. I told him and he gave his man a rollocking for being rude.

I don't really know to this day why those two big-name acts were such expensive flops. Perhaps it was partly due to my lack of promotional experience; perhaps the people of Carlisle just don't go for those kind of shows. After all, you do get towns in the country where speedway would never succeed. I had been warned in advance about the gamble of going into Carlisle with shows like this but I thought I knew better. Unfortunately, I didn't so it wasn't one of my better decisions.

I lost a few quid on Syd Lawrence but the one that put money in my pocket was Moira Anderson and I suspect a lot of people reading this won't have heard of her. She was attractive, a lovely singer and less expensive than the others. I was at the theatre in the afternoon of the show when an official from the Carlisle Crown Court walked in, introduced himself and asked if I was in charge. I thought twice about my answer and then said I was. His told me that a murder trial had ended suddenly when the accused had changed his plea so the judge, Mr Justice Caulfield, had a free evening. He was also a mad keen Moira Anderson fan and did I have any good tickets left. I thought: 'Just a few.' I always kept a couple of front row tickets in my back pocket for such events so I gave the official two and he said he would bring the judge along later.

Moira was in the dressing room when the official returned with the judge and introduced me to him. He was an extremely intimidating character but appeared to be a nice man and he thanked me for the front row seats. The official then asked me if there was any chance of his Honour meeting Miss Anderson so I said I would do my best to arrange it. I asked if I could do him a deal and said that if ever I appeared in front of him and was found guilty, would he be lenient with me? Not many people get the chance to say that to a judge and he passed it off.

I went backstage and explained to Miss Anderson that there was a High Court judge on the front row and would it be possible for him to meet her? She agreed and I took him in. He changed from being a judge to a fan and you would have thought I had given him the Crown jewels... well perhaps not the Crown jewels! He shook my hand so many times and I understand he sent her a bottle of champagne. So it was a memorable night and not just because it was the only time I made money in Carlisle.

27 – Then and Now

I WAS 27 when I started promoting at Workington. I knew my riding career was going nowhere slowly and, if I ever needed proof, it came on a trip down south with my pal 'Bandy' Burnett whose son, Paul, is riding at the moment.

We went to Rye House to have a spin after a meeting there and I picked up a second half booking at Wimbledon from Mr. Ronnie Greene the next night. We took a tent so we could stay over cheaply, found a field but could not get the tent up.

That was the only night of my life that I slept in a car. I woke up next morning surrounded by nosey cows. I sat there looking at them out of the window and thought: 'Is this what a speedway star does?'

I was going backwards but I couldn't bear the thought of not being involved in the sport I'd loved since I was a kid so I turned my attention to promoting and started a search for a track that led me to Workington.

That was 1970 and the sport has changed dramatically since then. In those days, unlike now, virtually every promoter was full-time and if he didn't make his track pay, he didn't eat on a Sunday.

There are very few, if any, genuine full-time promoters running speedway these days. Tony Mole and Terry Russell are probably the nearest but there are more consortiums about these days. Broadly speaking, every promoter was 100 per cent in the job when I started, now nobody is.

The costings of speedway in those days meant I used to need 3,000 people at my tracks to break even. Now there isn't a track in the country that can pull in that kind of figure, certainly on a regular basis.

When I opened at Workington the official pay rate for riders was 50p a start and 50p a point. That means he would earn £10 for a 15-point maximum. My rates were £1 a start and £1 a point and I was regarded as a big payer. I probably wrote in excess of 50 per cent of the rulebook – and broke a few of them! – and a fair proportion are still being used today.

I invented the Pairs and the Four Team tournament in those days and, I'm pleased to say, both of them are still running today although the Fours is only being held in the Premier League.

I thought up those competitions when I was at Newcastle and the basic reason was to find something else that the Diamonds could win because they were cleaning up everything in those days. The first Pairs event was at Belle Vue and Tom Owen and Brian Havelock won it for Newcastle.

I'm pleased that events I brought in all those years ago are still running and are still popular.

One of the best innovations to have been made in British speedway is the introduction of fixed gate positions. As a team manager, you always had problems with two riders wanting the same place. Inevitably, the better rider would get his way, which was hard on his team-mate who would have to go into a race at an even greater disadvantage.

The situation now with the fixed gate positions is much fairer. It has alleviated all the problems and made the team manager's job a lot easier.

Another thing I like now, as against when I started, is the bonus point for winning home and away league matches on aggregate. It's a brilliant idea although I do think it is overvalued. You only get a point, just the same as for a draw, and I feel that is worth more than a bonus point. An away draw is much harder to achieve.

I'd give three points for a win, two for a draw and keep one for the bonus point as it is at the moment. It is a contentious issue because a track with a big home advantage has a better chance of winning the league. People say bonus points were the big difference when Exeter won the championship because it is was easier for them to collect bonus points. Overall, I feel they are a good thing but I do think their importance should be diminished.

I know I will be accused of being old fashioned but I much prefer the one-off World Final to the Grand Prix system we have now. The old final had much more drama on the night, wherever it was being raced. It was so special but the 2005 Grand Prix was such an anti-climax because everyone virtually knew who was going to win it at the halfway stage and certainly before the end.

Everyone had to qualify for the old one-off final, wherever in the world he came from. There were no selected riders as there are now. The riders were there on merit because they had earned the chance and I feel the atmosphere and excitement of the old way has never been replaced.

In reality, a Grand Prix is only one of nine or ten qualifying rounds. The big stadiums appear to be dropping out of staging GPs and we had meetings last season at places like Malilla, in Sweden, with an

11,000 capacity. It's like soccer staging a big cup final at Bury with a semi-final at Gillingham.

It must be a cause of concern for the Grand Prix bosses at BSI as they don't seem to be getting the big stadium meetings that had been their original policy, although the British GP at Cardiff and the Polish rounds are obvious exceptions.

The Grand Prix system hasn't done our Elite League competition any good at all. Because of the GPs, and the leagues in Sweden and Poland in particular, it is very difficult to race here on a Saturday with only Eastbourne making it viable.

Few can race on a Friday because of GP practice and, if the meetings are in Slovenia or Poland, the top boys aren't keen on racing in England on Thursdays either because they are difficult venues to get to.

We can't use Sundays or Tuesdays for the Elite League because of the Polish and Swedish leagues so our options are being reduced all the time. The basis of running a track that is successful financially is continuity so the fans know what's happening and it is becoming harder and harder to achieve.

I feel there is no doubt that I am in the minority with my opinion of the Grand Prix system but, in a nutshell, it has always been my opinion that, in any sport, the public want to see the winner decided on the night.

Similarly, I'm not happy with the way the Elite League championship is decided these days. Last year it was run over a 36-match league programme and that should have been it with the side amassing the most points being declared the champions.

But now we have a league competition, only to decide the champions with a knockout cup event. It's very much a case of deciding a marathon with a sprint and it's ridiculous.

I know that we all know the rules of the competition at the start of the season and I know we have to adhere to them. But it doesn't make them right. In my view we don't have a league and a cup, we have two cups because both are decided on a knockout basis.

I know it puts a sting in the end of a season and gives TV a dramatic climax. But is it fair that a team who finish a fistful of points behind the top side in the league then win the championship? We all know the answer to that question is a resounding 'No.'

A lot of showmanship has gone out of speedway and I'm not talking about booking acts as added attractions, which I like to do. I've always been one to give my paying public a little extra now and again, although I never charge any extra so the people who only want to see the racing cannot complain they are paying for something they don't really want to watch.

For instance, in the old days when Boston came to Workington I used to give a bigger build-up to their promoter, Cyril Crane, than I did their team. He was a great character and you could always wind him up on some issue to the point where he would climb over the safety fence, run up through the crowd and burst into the referee's box. The fans loved it but if a promoter did it these days, he'd be fined or even banned.

I went back to Workington once when I was running Newcastle and John Whittaker, now the Clerk of the Course at Sheffield, was the referee. He was a top man on the buttons. I'd telephoned him to do my nut about something during the meeting and, while he was talking to me, an irate Workington fan had emptied a pint of beer over his head.

John was dripping. I said I hoped he was going to report it. He just said: "I never saw anything."And got on with the meeting.

It used to be part and parcel of the game that promoters could have a go at a referee but those days have gone. Last season I expressed a view in the Manchester Evening News that a referee had made two hometown decisions in a match at Coventry. I got a letter from the Speedway Control Bureau severely reprimanding me for criticising the official in public. The only reason I wasn't fined was because of my record for good conduct so I just got a warning.

In the old days, if you felt a decision or two had been a bit iffy you could tell the referee you were going out onto the centre green to jump about a bit to get the crowd going. If you did it now you would get fined. The old way was better because you could put on a show and get your fans involved. Perhaps someone can tell me what's wrong with that because it has taken some of the fun out of the sport.

Len Silver, Bill Bridgett and Johnnie Hoskins, who used to set fire to his hat, are other promoters who were also showmen and speedway is the poorer now the antics of yesteryear are frowned on.

When start time comes around I still use the phrase: 'Okay, let's get the show on the road'. Speedway, like soccer, cricket, any sport you like to mention, is not just a sport, it's entertainment, show business. They are basically the same things to me because a good match is a good show and, therefore, good entertainment. And that's what we are here for. Isn't it?

If people see a good match and go home happy, then we've done our job. Rugby League is a fair example of bringing showmanship back into their sport and I will be bringing in more additional attractions like I have done at my previous tracks.

It didn't happen last year because it was so hectic in our first season at Belle Vue and, let's be honest, we didn't need anything else for our opening night because we had the club's former World Champions, Ivan Mauger, Ove Fundin and Peter Collins, as our guests.

Entertainment is my keyword and there are so many things you can't do without getting into trouble.

I don't think riders need to be too accessible to the supporters because they've got their own lives to lead. Footballers aren't accessible and I don't think there is any harm in riders going into the bar occasionally after a match to rub shoulders with the fans.

But that's something else that has changed dramatically in recent years because so many of them are passing between different countries all the time. We always have riders from both sides coming into Belle Vue on a Monday from Poland and then flying straight out again to Sweden.

However, for all the changes in speedway over the years, the bottom line is that we still have four riders in a race, doing four laps and turning left at each corner.

Alan Dick, who is a co-promoter at Glasgow and a high-ranking official at Partick Thistle football club, is relatively new to speedway. He told me that in 50 years of football they've hardly changed any rules but in his three years of speedway, we've changed about 50.

I'm a great believer in not mending things that aren't broken but I fear we have been guilty of doing that in speedway. For instance, I am very much opposed to the tactical rider rule where the points count double. I think it makes it very difficult for us to be able to sell speedway as a credible sport to the media, the public and the sponsors. Perhaps people who complain about the sport's coverage would do well to consider that point.

It's like saying that if a football team goes so far behind any goal they score can count as two. It's just not acceptable. Do you think football would have a rule that if a team opted to take a penalty from twice as far back it would count double? The answer to that, of course, is no and we should be saying the same thing about this speedway rule. But I'm afraid I can't see it happening.

I've never liked any form of rider control in team building or the use of guests but I do accept that they are necessary evils. The double points tactical rule, however, is an unnecessary evil.

Wheels and Deals

The coverage of speedway in the national Press has diminished over the years but now we have much greater exposure on TV to compensate. The Internet is also available now and it is a very powerful tool, which can also be a very dangerous one. I can never understand why people go under so many different pseudonyms. I'm something of a computer illiterate but if I was putting opinions on the Internet I would put my proper name on the bottom of it.

I think it is disgraceful that people go onto the Net, rip some track or some rider to shreds, and then don't have the courage of their convictions to sign it properly. The opinions of those people aren't worth a light.

28 – Ian Thomas: where now?

WHEN Phil Rising asked me to do this book, I wasn't sure what to expect but, boy, has it brought back some memories.

I was told to aim for between 75,000 and 80,000 words but I can honestly say that if Phil had said 150,000 was the target, it wouldn't have been a problem.

I've attempted to write it as it happened and I'd like to thank Richard Frost, who has worked on the book with me. How on earth anyone can listen to me talk for hour after hour is beyond me but he's one of the old school and has done a great job.

But back to the name of the chapter, Where Now? I have a contract with Tony Mole to run Belle Vue until the end of 2007 and I have bookings for my magic act in the diary for 2008 so it seems I'll be keeping busy for a little while yet.

I get my bus pass next year and, with the number of penalty points I have on my driving licence, I'll probably need it.

People ask me if or when I'm going to retire while those who don't know me ask how long I've been retired already! I must look very old but, after the life I've led and the miles I've covered, perhaps that isn't too surprising.

They also ask me what I'll do when I do finally retire and I don't know the answer to that, other than to say that Dot and I will visit more overseas countries. Australia is top of the list because I've paid out for so many return airfares over the years and still haven't been there myself.

When people retire they usually turn to their hobbies but that doesn't apply to me because they are speedway racing and magic, which are what I've been making my living from for many years. As long as anyone is prepared to use my services, I reckon I'll just keep going so little will change.

Finally, my thanks to you for buying this book and taking the time to read it. I sincerely hope you have enjoyed it. But if I've upset anyone along the way, tough!

Wheels and Deals

Wheels and Deals

Index

Wheels and Deals

Ian Thomas, the only man to team manage England to a speedway Grand Slam.

Ian Thomas, the man who has employed some of racing's all-time greats like Barry Briggs and Ivan Mauger – and 'sold' Ole Olsen without the Dane ever riding for him.

Ian Thomas, the man who nearly lost everything and battled his way back from the brink.

Ian Thomas, the man who has seen it all and won it all during his 57 years' involvement with speedway.

Ian Thomas, the man who has promoted successfully indoors, outdoors, and even in the middle of the desert.

Ian Thomas, a practising magician who has pulled more than a few promotional rabbits out of his hat.

Ian Thomas teams up with top journalist Richard Frost to bring you the complete lowdown on a man who lives for wheels and deals...

WHEELS *and* DEALS

by Ian Thomas

A **speedway** **Producti**

ISBN 0-9552376

9 780955 237

£14.95